TRISHA'S
TRANSFORMATION

TRISHA'S TRANSFORMATION

BEAT THE BULGE
AND STILL INDULGE

TRISHA LEWIS

GILL BOOKS

Gill Books

Hume Avenue

Park West

Dublin 12

www.gillbooks.ie

Gill Books is an imprint of M.H. Gill and Co.

© Trisha Lewis 2020

9780717188680

Designed by Jane Matthews

Photography by Marc O'Sullivan and Monika Coghlan

Food styling by Charlotte O'Connell

Edited by Susan McKeever

Proofread by Emma Dunne

Indexed by Adam Pozner

Printed and Bound in Germany by Firmengruppe APPL

This book is typeset in Acumin Pro.

They say that you should never meet your heroes. Well, I am so lucky to meet mine every single day.

This book is for you, Mam. For being my strength when I was weak. No matter how many times I tell you I love you, I will always love you more. I am a strong woman because a strong woman raised me. Forever your favourite child, hands down …
Trisha

'A mother's love is the fuel that enables a normal human being to do what they thought was the impossible.'

About the author

One of nine girls, 31-year-old Trisha Lewis grew up on a dairy farm in County Limerick. In February 2018, she tipped the scales at 26 stone. Since then, she has successfully lost eight stone. Having studied Professional Cookery in CIT, Trisha is now Executive Head Chef at Jacobs on the Mall in Cork City. Her passion is food and she's always believed you can lose weight without losing flavour. Trisha is now on a mission to overcome obesity in the most public way possible – documenting her weight-loss journey on her Instagram page, @Trishas.transformation. With over 100,000 Instagram followers – lovingly known as her Transformers – Trisha is well and truly beating the bulge.

CONTENTS

Lucy's communion – It was my first time wearing a dress without tights!

The Jacobs gang.

My butter towers!

Doing some elevated squats in the gym.

Introduction

Hello! You have bought my book and that was your first mistake! Let me introduce myself. My name is Trisha Lewis and I run the Instagram page @trishas.transformation. I come seventh in a large family of nine sisters and I have 12 nieces and nephews, with another on the way.

When I was a young girl, I worked part-time in a restaurant at home called The Hunters Rest. The head chef Rob guided me and showed me how to cook and respect food from a young age. In a household of 11 there was always someone hungry, so I have always enjoyed feeding people. I started my professional cookery course in CIT and from there I got my job in the mad busy Cork restaurant Jacobs on the Mall. I'm now the Executive Head Chef there.

I am currently fighting the battle of beating the bulge, but I love my life – I spend most of my days smiling and having fun. My life hasn't always been amazing, though. When I stood on the scales in February 2018 and saw 26 stone on the display, I knew I had hit rock bottom. Since then I have lost 8 stone and each day, I am changing my life for the better.

I wanted to write this book to share my story – the ups and downs of a radical weight-loss programme. I wanted to help anyone who may have been in my position and show them that you have never gone too far. I have myself come from being depressed and not wanting to wake up to now going to sleep excited for the next day to dawn.

The recipes that I have chosen are simple, tasty and cost-effective. I picked them because I find the food you need to eat in the typical diets boring and non-sustainable. I would like to lose weight, but I do not want to lose flavour. I hope that people reading this book will be able to learn more about the old Trisha and hopefully follow in my footsteps. I hope that any reader who's been in my position will look at changing their lives with a positive attitude and fill their days with more laughter. It hasn't been the easiest thing baring my truth, but it has been so uplifting. Know that we are all in this mad life together. Let's be kind – not cruel. Let's move on from past mistakes and reset. Let's beat the bulge.

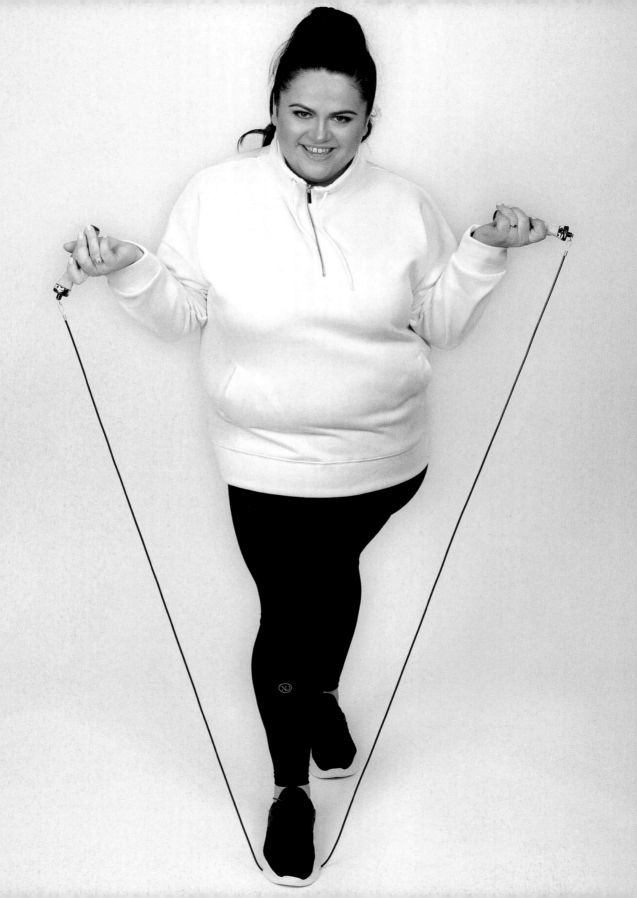

My STORY

Early signs

I have been sitting here for quite some time and I'm going to be honest. This is tough. Remembering the past and the negative side of it can be sometimes so difficult and it is still raw. What feelings do I feel when I think back? Hurt. Shame. Regret. Embarrassment.

I'll start from the very start. I grew up on a dairy farm in the countryside with my mam, dad and eight sisters. My dominant childhood memory of home is pure and utter craic. We spent our days playing games, setting up cubby houses, cycling, terrorising each other and giving Mam heart failure as we waved at her from the tallest tree we could find. We sat and we watched game shows, we told on each other when we caught each other cursing, we 'borrowed' items from each other's rooms. The house was full to the brim with unconditional love. Dad lived his life surrounded by 10 women and it's no surprise to any of us that he can't hear a thing. He was the man who taught me to read at three years of age and the man who from the very start of this journey has encouraged me. He stayed at home to milk the cows so Mam could come to *The Late Late Show* with me (for more on that see page 52)! He has always been there for me, through thick and thin. As for my mam, she's the best mother in the world and also my best friend and I am so grateful to have her in my life. She is one in a million and always puts her daughters before herself – a true superhero!

I guess when I look back now the signs were always there that I was an overeater. When I was six years old, I experienced raw pain for the first time when I lost my beloved nana. I know that I associated Nana with food – my earliest memory is sitting on the swing with a big box of Pringles as I convinced nana I was too sick to go to school. She always overruled Mam! Another memory I have is of me being in Nana's kitchen where she gave me a Black Jack bar. After a few minutes of chewing I turned to her and showed her my black tongue and I told her I was dying. She freaked out! The poor woman was 82 and terrified that she had poisoned me. I nearly choked laughing. Every morning I'd wake up and race up to Nana's house where she lived with my aunt Babe and my uncle Ned. I would go straight in and I would close the curtains, unplug the phone from the wall and make Nana sit down while I operated an incredibly busy call centre where she had to call out all the numbers from the phone book. The woman had the patience of a saint and adored the ground I walked on. To this day when I dial numbers at work, I never need to look at the keypad after my intense training as a four-year-old. Once my busy morning was over, we would sit down and she would feed me my dinner of spuds, boiled chicken and Hot Cup soup. After dinner I would raid her sweet press and eat chocolate and drink ginger ale while watching *The Den* and cuddling up to her and her dogs. I can safely identify that here is where my problems with having a huge appetite started. I would go back down home, and I would never tell Mam that I had eaten at Nana's and I would sit down and have another dinner.

When I lost Nana, I still kept up my eating habits as that felt like my secret normal. Whenever Mam would put up dinner, I would always heap my plate and take as much as I could. There was never a shortage of food, but I always had a sense of panic that I wouldn't have enough because I was missing out on Nana's dinners. Many a time I would grab an extra spud and eat it secretly. When I was in secondary school, I would try and get up earlier than my next older sister Annie to cook sausages for breakfast – but I would put on an extra two or three for me and gobble them before she came down. My biggest problem all my life has been secret eating like this. **When the phrase, 'The food you eat in secret you wear in public' was said to me it gave me such a land because it literally described me and my past.**

Schooldays and bullying

Over the years I knew that my weight was growing. I distinctly remember sneaking onto the scales when I was 10 years old. My sister Michelle had told me that whatever age you are should be your weight, so if you were six you should be six stone, etc. I recall feeling panicked when I saw 11 stone on the scales. When I was in primary school people first started telling me that I was fat. When the word 'fat' is first used, everything changes. You lose the carefree feeling of childhood and things are never simple again. You gain an anxiety around the word fat that will never go, and you will always fear it as a weapon. The first time I was called fat, we were playing a game of soccer at school. I tackled someone a bit too roughly and floored him. I remember being so shocked when he was like, 'Calm down, you fat animal.' I burned up with embarrassment. Kids will be kids and this stuff happens. One of my sisters had heard it said to me and told Mam. She sat me down and I remember crying to her that it had hurt me. Before school every day I would tear off down the road and get a bit of a walk in and then Mam would collect me, and we would strike off to school. This did eventually stop, and I don't remember why.

I was never really bullied too badly. Elements of it popped up but by the time it could have gotten worse I had found a way around it – and that was by either fighting or being the class clown. A few moments from my school years stand out. I went to one of the girls' houses when I was nine, I reckon. We all went to the local Mill River and we were going swimming. I had a navy swimsuit on with a red and white stripe down the side. I raced into the river, but the others strangely didn't follow. There was a group of eight of us – boys and girls. They stood at the edge of the river firing rocks at me, laughing at me and calling me fat. I remember being so upset but I said nothing. I laughed it off and tried my best to make them like me.

WHEN THE WORD FAT IS FIRST USED *everything* CHANGES!

For a few months this group of girls bullied me by scratching my name in the walls of the cubicles and calling me fat. As I sat on the loo, I read words like 'ugly', 'fat' and 'pig'. I kept this a secret from my mother and eventually told the teacher, who got the walls painted, and it stopped. I wish I had told my mother now as I can identify that was the beginning of keeping the word 'fat' a secret.

Once the older kids in the clique left the school, I became top dog and I started to lash out at the other girls. I started picking fights and getting revenge for the previous two years. I would start some serious physical fights because I truly hated them for what they had done to me. It got very serious and the parents got involved. I then admitted to my mother in floods of tears outside the school gate what had been happening. She knew her daughter and how unusual my reaction was and had my back 100 per cent in the whole thing. I swore to myself that I would never let anyone get the better of me again. I became very bold around this time. I wish I could let it go now, but when I see some of them, I get anxiety and this is over 20 years later.

Did I feel like the fat sister growing up? No, I didn't. I felt equal and I felt just as special as everyone else. Did that feeling stay? Sadly not. Through no fault of my family's, as the years passed, I felt myself becoming more and more estranged from them. My sisters never called me fat. They never mocked me. To be honest, I was the lunatic of the house and I spent every waking hour trying to annoy them. I was the alpha and hiding the Sky card was a special skill of mine when I didn't get my own way. I think it would be so much easier to understand why I became morbidly obese if I'd had a family that were cruel, but they were the complete opposite. They always had my back.

The day I signed my book contract.

I always felt so different inside and I now wish that I had spoken to my sisters. They would have helped me if I'd told them. I wish I could go back now and give myself this advice because back then the problem was so small.

I was always conscious of my weight compared to other people's. I knew I was fat for years. I didn't join any sports outside of school; I didn't want to be the fat one. I was always paranoid things wouldn't fit me. Helmets, jerseys and shorts. It was just easier not to do them. Now I love the gym so much I'm kicking myself – if I could go back, I would join every sport my sisters joined. **I love exercise and I know I would have been an Olympian if I had given myself the chance and gotten out of my own way.**

Five weddings

As the years went by my weight started to affect me and my sisters in other ways too. I was my sister's bridesmaid and I was so excited, I felt that this would be a push for me to lose weight. But the closer the day loomed, I just buried my head in the sand more and more. When it came to the dress fitting, I hated it. My dress had straps and no one else had them; it also had to get a minimiser bra built into it. I still smiled and told my family how happy I was.

That night at the reception I was so uncomfortable that I decided to bring my niece Eva to bed at 10 p.m. and just call it a night. Fast-forward a few years and another sister got engaged. I knew it was coming. I knew I was going to be asked. When Maura asked, I should have just said a straight-out no. I was about 6 stone heavier than the previous wedding and about a hundred times more depressed. I let the weeks go by and I ignored texts and calls about dress fittings; I left WhatsApp groups about hen nights. I was completely and utterly riddled with anxiety. I didn't want to be the fat sister on the altar again. I didn't want people to look up and see that I was three times bigger than the rest of the bridesmaids.

About a month before the wedding I walked into another sister's room and I broke down. I told Juliette that I didn't want to do it. She calmed me down and told me it didn't matter – all Maura wanted was me there, so Juliette agreed to take my place as bridesmaid. Weight had won again by taking another special memory from me.

When Annie got engaged, I just said, 'Don't ask me!' When your sibling gets married, it's a special time. I should have spent weeks planning my outfit and picking my shoes and getting excited. Instead before both

Me and my sister Carol.

weddings in 2015 I got my dress the day before. I knew my sisters were panicking but I knew in my heart of hearts that it would just be the size I was going for, not the style, so whatever fitted me, I bought. I didn't want to dress up. I just wanted both days to end so I could go back to being alone and sad. I remember walking into Evans and just picking up a big, black dress for both occasions and that was it. When it came to the family photo I blended into the background and tried to stand behind someone. I have had five sisters get married and for four of those weddings I wore a big black dress. If I had my time back again, I would go to every coffee date, every dress fitting, I would run the roads with them and I would smile bigger than any sister in the photo. **If you are reading this now and you can identify with any part of this, trust me when I say, just talk to your loved ones, they will help.**

My sisterhood

My sisters would always let me walk into a restaurant first and pick the table and the chair because they knew I was paranoid I wouldn't fit or the chair would break. Whenever I dropped something on the ground they would nearly get whiplash diving down to pick it up for me as they knew I couldn't. As much as I felt the stares walking down the street, they felt them too. They have told me of the sleepless nights they had, the hours of chats and trying to figure out how to help me. The saddest part of all this is I was so down I truly believed that they didn't care about me. I used often think how unfair life was. I often wished I was one of them. I felt like a burden. I would lash out at them as they were the closest people to me. I would tell them I hated them. In my lowest of moments, I told them I wished that I wasn't alive.

They took every single bit of abuse as they knew that I was suffering and that I couldn't see the wood for the trees. Each time I started a new diet, I would tell them and they would praise me, tell me how brilliant I was. Our WhatsApp group would be absolutely lit with excitement and support. Then silence would come from my end. I would have given up and they were always left with the harsh blue double tick of a message that had been read but not replied to. It was easier to make them uncomfortable than admit defeat once again.

Over the years I lost out on special moments with my sisters. I lost out on precious selfies. I lashed out. I fought with them. Now things are changing. I am sitting beside them and I'm enjoying the moment instead of calling myself names in secret. I am standing proud beside my army of sisters.

IN MY DARKEST MOMENTS, WHEN I THOUGHT I WAS ALONE, MY FAMILY WERE carrying me

My sisters have always been my greatest supporters. A number of years ago, when we were on holidays in Murcia, a guy approached me outside the club and asked me on a date. I knew instantly where it was going and he was like, 'We can go to McDonald's – you probably have a discount there for being their best customer!' I walked away and over to my two sisters with tears spilling down my face and they went back and instead of confronting him they went to his friends and they explained what he had done. They told them what kind of sister I was, the kind things I do for them, and the friends made the guy say sorry to me. But his words had got to me. The next night I downed all the alcohol in sight and ended up being aggressive and angry, lashing out at my sisters and spending the night trying to run away from them. God love them in a foreign country and I was like a wild animal trying to dodge them. I started arguing with them purely because I was so hurt from the night before. I was eventually put to bed after hours of them trying to corner me to get me into a cab and I fell asleep in floods of tears.

The next day as I lay on the patio sweating out alcohol in the hot Spanish sun, my sisters were so mad at me that they took off to the beach. While they were gone, I dragged myself off the red-hot terracotta tiles and I wandered to a local pound shop where I picked up some Halloween teeth. When we boarded the plane, they were still angry at me and I was being given the silent treatment so to break the ice I popped in the teeth and I turned to them and asked them to be my friend. The roars of laughter filled the Ryanair flight and all was right again!

I now know that my weight affected each and every one of them. They were in a constant state of worry and despair. They tried everything. They tried to be good cop, bad cop, fitness cop, healthy eating cop, Zumba cop, but alas nothing worked. Towards the end I know they made a decision to just be there and catch me when I fell because they were so scared, given how bad my mental health was, that I would push myself away from them completely. My sisters never ever gave up on me, they always believed that I would pull this out of the bag. They always held onto hope that their wild happy sister would come back.

With all my sisters I have been so lucky to have the best brothers-in-law. They have the same attitude and are constantly proud of me. One of them is Kev. Kev is my friend first and Jewel's boyfriend second. From the moment I decided to change my life he has been on the sidelines cheering me on, reining my notions back in and always knowing that I will smash it. He has spoken to me at length about my transformation. They lived in London and each time they came home I was always bigger but I was never judged. He still treated me with love. Three months into my journey we went for an Indian in London and we jogged home. It was something small, the rain was pouring down as we slowly made our way home but my eyes were brimming with tears of joy. It was a moment that stands out for me because for the first time in a long time I felt normal and proud. I was jogging for the first time in years. They left for Melbourne recently and I just cannot wait to make him uncomfortable with my cockiness in a bathing suit when I visit them in 2020!

I have an army of nieces and nephews who are all so, so important to me. In this army I have two very important small men and I need to be the good influence that they deserve: Jack and Danny. I was blessed to be asked to be their godmother and I adore them both. The bond that I hold with them is so special. Jack – you are just my absolute sweetheart. Our little chats I will always hold dear, you are so proud of me and you are just the best little boy in the world. You and Danny, my two Man United supporters, mean the world to me. I have

The main men!
My godchildren,
Danny and Jack.

heard your request and I will not have any more godchildren. Together we are going to have the most fun and someday I will bring you both to Old Trafford and thank you for being the best godchildren I could ask for. The rest of ye pups – Eva, Eoghain, Will, Pearse, Amy, Lucy, Oran, Dylan, Luke and Dean – know that I adore you all so much and I will forever be the bold aunt!

The shame of being fat-shamed

Fat-shaming is a very popular discussion now. A lot of people agree with it and just as many don't. You can dress it up and say it is helping people and that it is coming from a good place but until you feel the harsh burn of a name being called at you or when your ears hear the cruel laughter from a group of people mocking your weight, I really don't think you can or should have an opinion on this matter.

I've had my fair share of cruel comments over the years, but it really picked up speed the more weight I gained and the more vulnerable I became. I think the worst feeling in the world is being laughed at and not feeling good enough. Towards the end and before my transformation began, I had decided to avoid any social situation as I was so sick and tired of being the fattest person in every room. It's a hard thing to notice as you quickly glance around the room. Fat-shaming just reaffirms what you are already telling yourself: that you are disgusting, fat, gross and unlovable. It's been happening me since I was 10 years of age

Once you've reached a certain weight bracket, I feel that people think you are fair game. Countless nights out ended in tears for me and I constantly kicked myself for even bothering to go out. One night I was out with my friends after work – at that point I was Head Chef in Jacobs on the Mall. There was the usual carry on – we would go to Crane Lane bar and sit in the smoking area on the long bench where my back would be to a wall and I wasn't in the way. As I sat in my seat watching people have fun, my friends went to the bar to get more drinks. I was sitting on my tod not bothering with anyone when a young handsome man approached me and sat in the chair across from me. He simply asked me for a lighter and I obliged. He asked me my name and a few other mindless questions. My gut was sending me warning signals – I knew a guy like that wasn't speaking to me for anything other than to mock me, I was silently wishing my friends Niamh and Colm would hurry back.

After a few seconds he whipped out his phone and asked me for my number. I didn't move as I was frozen with fear. I knew what I looked like and I knew that he wasn't being serious. He slid the phone across the table and before it reached my trembling hand, he stopped it and picked it back up. He then giggled and looked back at the group of lads that were standing nearby with their phones out filming their friend chatting up the fat girl. He turned to me and smirked: 'Jesus, my bad, I don't want your number – you're a fat bitch!'

Now in hindsight I should have asked him why he did that to me, I should have marched straight over to my friends and told them that this guy had hurt me but instead what I did was transform his cruelty to me into guilt and shame. I deserved that because I was fat. I simply did an Irish goodbye and slipped from the pub leaving an empty table while the sounds of his friends' laughter echoed in my ears. I went home that night like most nights and sobbed into my pillow. I felt trapped in fat prison.

Another night I was out again with my work gang and left them at about 11 o'clock as they were heading to a lively bar I knew I would hate to be in. I headed to the local pizza place and I ordered two slices of pizza. The guy behind the counter started to pull two whole pizzas from the cabinet. I presumed that he had misheard me but sadly he hadn't; he thought he was being funny. He told me to come on, surely I would eat two whole pizzas. I remember looking at him and asking him why would he do that to me? A lady in the queue was so angry and defended me but I walked out as I couldn't take the shame anymore. I happened to bump into my sister Kellie – I don't know what would have happened if I hadn't met her. She was horrified at my tears and she asked me what had made me so upset. I usually hid this pain from them, but she caught me at a low moment. I told her what he had said, and she went in and told him he should be ashamed of himself; I was the nicest sister and the kindest woman to walk the streets and why would he hurt her sister like that? It didn't matter at that stage; I was so mortified, I just wanted the ground to swallow me.

Recently at 100 lb down I decided that I would get a spray tan. As you girls will know, you are instructed to wear loose clothing to avoid marks on your tan. I did as I was instructed, and I wore a lovely navy cotton dress that was above the knee. I met my niece Eva for sushi before work and as we exited the restaurant, I knew what was coming. Three women were standing on the path with a buggy and three small kids. They immediately focused on me and started laughing. Eva, who had never seen this type of behaviour, didn't cop anything so I quickly picked up my pace to head as far away as I could from these women. From behind they bellowed that I was a fat pig, I should cover myself up and that I was disgusting. I felt so bad for my niece who was horrified and scared and confused as to why this was happening. She stopped to go back and speak to the women, but I begged her to keep going, it would just make it worse. As we walked up the South Mall her little face fell as she told me how angry she was for me, how she had never witnessed this type of behaviour before and she said she was sorry she didn't do more. I simply told her to not worry about it – just don't ever be like those girls. We hugged it out and yes it did hurt but it wasn't painful. I know that I am on the road to being happy and those girls will never know what it's like to feel like I feel. **I cannot change the behaviours of others, but I can change how I react.**

I have been called fat from passing cars, people have asked me when my calf was due, I have been taunted with terms like 'wide load coming.' I have lost count of the nights that I have had some comment passed at me. What I will never lose is the feeling I will always carry from those nights: hurt, shame and disgust. **Trust me when I say this, fat-shaming does not and will never lead to a healthy weight-loss attempt by the victim.** It will either riddle you into months of shame and self-disgust or it will propel you to lose as much weight as possible in a non-sustainable way. There are some people in this world who will never understand weight and will always think that it is okay to laugh and mock someone who has more body fat than them. Only recently the same guy who threw the rocks at me when I was swimming saw me at a live podcast and started to snigger and point at me to his friends. Twenty years on Trisha Lewis being fat is still funny. But now I've decided that I will no longer be a punching bag for the uneducated.

If you are reading this and you have children, don't even mention weight to them. Don't mention size. Let the children learn that someone's soul is so much more beautiful than their waistline. Let them know that it is wrong to mock. If someone is making comments about your weight, stop them. Report them. Don't make the mistake I did and let it fester. You can't change the person that hurt you, but you can change you. Don't lose weight from anger at what someone said to you – lose weight for you. Move on and always remember hurt people tend to hurt people. **Accepting I was fat and learning to love myself has been the best thing that I have ever done.** Since nine years of age I have given the word fat so much power. It is time for me to realise that it is a silly word. It isn't who I am or who I will become. I am not over the fat-shaming; I am still a target, but I plan on grabbing and keeping every single brick that is fired at me in the past and the future and I will build my kingdom from it.

SOMEONE'S SOUL IS SO MUCH MORE *beautiful* THAN THEIR WAISTLINE.

Seatbelt extensions and sweaty holidays

Everyone loves holidays – going on holidays you are excited. You know that you will switch off for the week. You will feel the sun on your bones and parts of your skin will appear that never see the light of day. You will wear colours you wouldn't dare wear at home. You will wear no makeup and feel light and free. But for me it was the complete opposite, another occasion when I was terrified of opportunities for people to fat-shame me. I'd get so excited for a holiday when it was booked but as the weeks approached my stomach would fill with the usual sense of dread and anxiety. I always waited until the day before leaving to shop for clothes, picking up random pieces I hoped would fit. The first time that I realised I needed a seatbelt extension was when I went on a school tour to Switzerland when I was 13. Instead of asking for one, I became a pro at covering my unfastened belt with my top or tucking it into the top of my pants. I always felt such relief when the air hostess walked on after checking my row. Over the years a familiar dread would fill my bones as I walked up the steps to the aircraft. I was always afraid of being caught out. On a flight to Edinburgh as I sat beside my friend the mortifying moment happened where the air hostess asked to see my buckle. She knew that the belt couldn't fit me so she caught me. I remember burning up with fear, my secret was out. My friend didn't take a blind bit of notice as we were off on a fun weekend. Either John didn't cop it or he pretended not to – I must ask him!

I became very cunning at checking in for flights. I would always pay for the window seat so I wasn't blocking anyone in and no matter how long the flight was I would never, ever go to the toilet. I would always check my friends into different seats and pay the extra tariff. I didn't want them to see me ask for the dreaded orange belt. They knew I needed one but I was oblivious. I would always subtly ask the staff when I boarded the flight in the hope that they would open the drawer and give it to me there and then. Sometimes they did, other times they didn't. As I sat in my seat trying not to grimace at the handle digging into my side the air hostess would start walking towards me holding the orange belt, and at that stage the whole flight knew who the fat girl was who needed a seatbelt extension.

One summer me and my friend Colm decided to go on a 10-day trip to three destinations in Europe. We spent the whole trip laughing and making memories I will always hold dear, but it was also fraught with stress and pain. Colm never once looked at my weight but became my friend through sheer craic and laughter. I remember one night in Crane Lane he had a chat with me and said that I was so lovely but it would be great if I could join a gym with him and we could train together. It didn't hurt, it was so comforting to drunkenly hope that I would change my life in the morning. I think we went for chicken wings instead of squats after – but he tried!

We spent the first three days drinking mojitos and staying in awful hostels in Paris. I was so out of my comfort zone of hotels – it wasn't even funny – but when you have your friend it doesn't matter in the slightest.

We laughed around Paris **but inside I was struggling so bad.**

Colm walked the length and the breadth of the city and I didn't want to feel different so I kept going. It was so warm and I was constantly out of breath. My legs were chafing uncomfortably, I was never not roasting. It was so stressful. One day we went sightseeing and we travelled to Sacré-Coeur to the hilltop in Montmartre. The Metro wasn't working for that particular stop so we started to walk up the steep streets to the base of the steps that would lead us to this church. I was 25 stone and feeling fairly unfit. A small restaurant hidden by trees and branches was positioned at the foot of these steps and I convinced Colm to have a coffee. The main reason I remember was because I was already exhausted from the walk through the streets of Paris. The number of stairs to this church is three hundred. Three hundred steps up. By the time I got to the top I was so dizzy and out of breath I didn't care about the church. I was too busy blinking to stop seeing stars but I didn't give up. We started off together and after the seventh flight I told Colm to flake on, I would meet him at the top. About 40 minutes later I joined him. I hated every single second of it and I was so angry that I was like this. Old people were shooting past me as I puffed and wheezed and held onto the rail pretending to look at my phone.

Leaving Paris, we hopped on a flight to our next destination, Rome. One of my tricks was I would always board the flight nearly last so I didn't have to be on the flight for too long. I was ecstatic when I realised my row had three free seats. I wasn't sitting beside anyone. This was the best day ever. I sat in and started to make myself as comfortable as I could in the tiny seat. A couple started to approach. As they got closer my stomach fell and so did their faces. It was a young couple. They sat down and they made it very clear from the start that they were allergic to sitting beside me. The lady started elbowing me and huffing and puffing and making all kinds of drama. She swapped with her partner and he sat beside me. At this stage I was trying to make myself as small as possible up against the window and if I could have opened the window, I would have jumped out of it. After what felt like an eternity, they pressed the buzzer for an air hostess to come down.

I knew in my gut that what I always feared was about to happen. The air hostess arrived down and the lady started to complain in the loudest voice. She said that it wasn't fair she had paid for a seat and it was disgusting that I was spilling over the seats. I should be made pay for their seats as they were uncomfortable. For some reason the hardest part of the whole scene for me was the air hostess. I strangely felt so alone as I thought that she might stick up for me but she responded that she completely understood and she would see what she could do. At this stage when she walked away my head was turned out the window and tears burned my eyes. After what felt like eternity she came back and moved the couple. I do understand that you need comfort on a flight. I just wish that the people were kinder in their approach. I wasn't made of stone – I was made of many stones but not stone. After that I swore I would either not go on a holiday or book two seats. I wish I could go back and tell that couple that what they did was mean, it was unnecessary dramatics and it hurt like hell.

I decided on that flight to take a video of myself showing myself how disgusting I was. To this day I don't know why I took the video, I think in one way I hoped that it would be my 'before' video but I honestly think I took it to torture myself more and remind myself how truly disgusting I was. I cried the entire flight, but by the time I stepped off the plane the demons had convinced me to shut up, tell no one and continue on. The first time my friend Colm, who was oblivious that this had happened, found out about this was when he watched *The Late Late Show* in January 2019.

The gastric bypass saga

In 2016 after years of reading about gastric bypasses and surgeries, I finally felt that it was my only option – I was so heavy, I was barely able to walk. I remember keeping it a secret as I emailed the surgery back and forth. I had a strange feeling of shame. I felt that everyone would tell me that I was taking the easy way out. In fact, it was one of the hardest things to admit to my loved ones, that I had to get my stomach cut in half in order to fix myself. If anyone tells you that it is the easy way out, they haven't walked a second in your shoes. It was the scariest and most heart-breaking decision that I have ever made.

I researched getting the surgery done in Cork and my heart sank when I found it could cost up to €22,000. I looked up getting loans from the bank. I then decided that I would go abroad as it was €14,000 cheaper to get it done in Belgium. I eventually told my family what I was planning, and by this stage, my mind was made up so they had no choice but to support me. **This is the side of obesity that isn't spoken about.** Sometimes your family are so frightened of losing you that whenever you get a small glimmer of hope they hold onto that too. They understood why I was doing it. What I know now is that behind the scenes they were at their wits' end and were absolutely petrified. I went into work and my heart was soaring with happiness; I would no longer be fat. I filled in my friend and my boss Michelle and we made a plan that we would make the trip to Dublin for the initial appointment as much fun as we possibly could. This was going to be the last trip that I was going to feel depressed and ugly on.

I made my way to Douglas and I got a blow dry across from Michelle's house. I took a photo of my stomach that day in the chair and I was so happy as I imagined that this would be my 'before' photo someday. We rang the Croke Park Hotel and we booked a night there and then we decided that we would treat ourselves to a fancy dinner. It's gas now when I look back … I was ringing the restaurant from the car on the way up and the only booking we could get was for 9.30 p.m. that night. I was so delighted internally because it would mean that we had less of a chance of going to a bar after and my anxiety was instantly reduced. I wish now that I had turned to Michelle and told her all of that but I kept it hidden. When we landed at the hotel, we had twin beds. This may seem like a minute detail. To me, it was everything. It meant that I didn't have to share a bed and spend the night awake panicking that I was taking over most of the bed, or that my breathing would have been too loud.

The last time I had been in Dublin prior to this trip was to see Beyoncé and I remember being in the bathroom and feeling so sad that I wasn't getting glammed up; I wasn't jumping into the shower; I was changing one large black top for another. In a matter of 18 months I felt like I had aged 80 years. We headed out to Fade Street Social for dinner and it was gorgeous. I remember thinking that this was going to be one of the last meals that I'd have feeling like this. After the surgery, I would have to eat small, light dishes, so I decided that I would order another starter on top of my three-course meal. I remember ordering 12 oysters – six cooked and six uncooked. I can now identify that as my 'self-destruct' button.

Internally, I was crying and I wanted to punish myself for going this far. That is where the majority of the overeating towards the end actually came from. It came from my feeling of absolute self-disgust; I wanted to match how my head felt by being over-full. We headed home after the meal and it was time to sleep. I can honestly say that it was the worst night's sleep I have ever had. I spent the night panicking, crippled with anxiety, so upset that I was this girl. I was finally this girl. The one I used to read about in magazines but always had the comfort in knowing that I hadn't gone that far. Well now, I had. I was so angry with myself. I was angry with the world. I didn't want to be obese. We headed off to a shopping centre in Malahide where the meeting was taking place in one of the rooms there. I remember being so excited, that this was the beginning of the end. My suffering was going to stop

When we arrived at the shopping centre, I took a video. I am so grateful I have that video. It is a glimpse into my past. When I watch that video, my heart swells with sadness. I can see a girl. A girl who I know very well but has become a stranger to me. A girl who I wish I could reach into the camera and tell her that it's going to be okay. A girl who is wearing pink socks that are so visible but she doesn't care because her feet are so swollen it is stopping the pain of her shoes cutting her. I see a girl who is so tired. We went into a packed waiting area where people all had extreme weight problems. I remember looking around and, honestly, I was thinking these poor people have so much weight. After about 20 minutes I asked Michelle did I look like these people? I know this seems like a strange question when I was in the same waiting room for a gastric bypass, but you really want the answer to be 'no'. She turned to me and she asked me did I want her to be honest? My heart sank and I said 'yes'. **She then told me that I was bigger than everyone in the room.**

It was so scary to hear that. That morning, I had grabbed a pencil and a notepad from the hotel and Michelle had made me write down a list of questions that she was concerned about. With my notepad and my pencil, I headed into the consultation room where I was greeted by the surgeon's secretary. Up until this point the only contact I had had with this company was when I had emailed them and explained my situation. I was then forwarded on a medical questionnaire and I filled that out. The very next email contained a list of dates when I could book the surgery. I had asked questions about the recovery period in the email and they had gone unanswered, so I just assumed they would be answered on the day.

I should have taken this as *a huge warning sign.*

The consultation time was 10 minutes. I was popped up on the weight scales and my weight read as 170 kg. I was then told that I would need to lose 5 kg so that the surgery could go ahead. I started to ask the questions and the guy told me to pop them in an email and they would come back to me. I remember telling this to my sisters and they were so concerned, but I basically told them that I was doing it and that was it.

The advice that the secretary gave me was to join an online Facebook forum where they had all their previous patients and they would provide me with some insight. Here I was, invited into a secret world of before and afters. People were losing stones and stones and their lives were changing. I was glued to the success of these patients. I think that I subconsciously chose not to read the negative posts, and just the before and afters. I spent hours at night going onto these people's pages and looking at their progress and dreaming up a new life for myself.

I am still a member of this group, and sadly things are taking a slightly sinister turn for the worse for its members. Now, the forum is filled with words like dumping, diarrhoea, reflux, kidney stones. People are reporting a lack in vitamin B12, their hair is falling out, surgeries for skin removals are being booked and revisions are happening more than actual surgeries. People's emotions and heads are wrecked as weight gain seems to creep back in. I am reading horror stories of bands eroding and people regaining what they lost, and more.

On the way home, we stopped in Kildare Village and I remember being in the Ugg store as slippers were the only thing that fit me and, ironically, they didn't have my size in stock so I went home empty-handed. I sat outside on a bench and I remember looking around and smiling as I knew that someday in the future I would come here and I would shop. Someday I would walk from these stores laden down with bags. I would be wearing nice clothes. I wouldn't be out of breath. I wouldn't be depressed. I wouldn't just spend money in the restaurant. Three years later, the next time I stepped foot into Kildare Village was to meet Sarah from Gill Publishing to sign the contract on my first ever book about my weight loss. I wore a navy dress with some high-heeled sandals: my legs were out! It had strangely worked out for me. I sat in a restaurant with Annie by my side. I was back in Kildare Village and my wish had come true. I was happy. I was alive. There is always a silver lining. But more on that later.

That evening when we were back in Cork I excitedly told my family about it on the phone. The same recurring questions came in so I decided that I would write an email to the secretary for some more insight. I asked things like

- **Is there a pre-op and a post-op diet?**
- **Will I be advised on what calories I will have to consume?**
- **Is one of the side-effects after these surgeries really alcoholism?**

The answers were short and curt. My biggest fear was of the alcoholism. I have a very addictive personality by nature and I had read this over and over again. The response that was given to that question was that no patients use the surgery as an excuse for alcoholism. Even after all these doubts, I booked my surgery for 15 March 2017. I had been sent on a list of dates and told to pick one. It was the shortest email ever.

I booked my flights with Aer Lingus and I fought and argued with my whole family that I wanted to do this alone. I remember my sister Michelle crying that she was going, end of, and if I ignored her for the five days, she didn't care; she was coming over with me. I spent my next few months chatting with people about my surgery and telling them how excited I was.

What I should have done was tell them I was terrified. I was uneasy. I was scared this was going to kill me. I felt that I couldn't ask the clinic as they didn't seem to have the time to answer me. The reason I didn't turn to my family and tell them was because I was sick of failing.

I was tired of always *letting them down.*

New starts and new cars

In February of 2017, I purchased a brand-new car and a pair of designer sunglasses. It was going to be the year of new starts and beginnings. As I drove my new Polo into my hometown my sister Annie called me and I answered on my brand-new Bluetooth in my fancy car! I told her I would meet her on the main street. When I pulled up, I was so delighted to show off my new car and my glasses. We did a mini photo shoot of her and the glasses and I convinced her she needed them. We sat into the car and were chatting about all its class features. As I was boasting about my electric windows Annie had stopped talking. She then said that she needed to talk to me. That all of the family were worried I wasn't thinking this through properly.

She told me that she believed in me and I will never forget the line she said: 'If you can walk onto a plane and do this surgery – you can walk into a gym, and try one last time.' She told me that I would lose who I was. Food was my passion. Food was my career. As I listened, I was panicked but I knew she was right. That was the line that drove it home and made me admit to her that I wanted to cancel – it was the straw that broke the camel's back. 'When you go to Marbella you can't have prawns pil pil cause the oil will separate and could kill you.' She completely made that up and I remember crying, telling her that if I didn't do this, I was afraid of what was in store for me. She told me to leave the money off – it was only money. I'd known from the start that the deposit was non-refundable. When I spoke to all my sisters after, they were all so relieved and happy with my decision.

Over the next year, it was a tough road as I continued to gain weight and I turned to the familiar emotion: blame. I was so angry at Annie and my sisters for making me back out. I cried in anger at them that I would

Marty Guilfoyle and me laughing and having fun, as usual. How I wish I had Sally Hansen-ed those legs!

have been fine. Why did they stop me? They had ruined any hope of me having a family and happiness. Hindsight is a beautiful thing. My sisters were right all along. They had to deal with the brunt of my anger, but because they loved me and could see the pain that I was in, they tolerated my anger. It's something that I still feel guilty about. **I hurt them because I was hurting.**

Rock bottom and my lightbulb moment

I think that the idea of a lightbulb moment is sold to us incorrectly. I always expected my lightbulb moment to be glamorous. That the minute it switched on I would be fixed and all my worries would go away. The truth is that rock bottom isn't a very Hollywood place to be. There is no bright light. There is no eureka moment. There is no one but you in a very dark, lonely place. When the lightbulb switches on it is only for a second and you're then left alone with the challenge of your own thoughts. The battle begins. I like to describe my journey as similar to stepping into someone else's house. You haven't a clue where anything is and it is all strange to you. Nothing is familiar. I would like you to imagine that this house is pitch black and you have to navigate your way around in the dark. You are scared. You think that every step you take you will trip and fall. There are demons hiding everywhere and they are shouting at you to give up, telling you to turn back and go home to what you know. They are telling you will never find the light switch. They are screaming at you that you will fail. They are laughing at you, telling you that you don't belong here. Eventually after days of searching and thousands of moments wanting to give up, you find a tiny match. It gives you a small glimpse into what this house looks like. It makes your journey a small bit easier.

Day after day you find new ways of filling the house with light until eventually you switch on the giant chandelier at the top of the stairs. It took you months to find the switch but through sheer grit and determination you find it. This is exactly how my 'lightbulb moment' felt. I was at my wits' end. Rock bottom had jumped up and hit me in the face. My cards were face up for the world to see. I was morbidly obese and depressed.

MY CARDS WERE FACE UP FOR THE WORLD TO SEE. I WAS MORBIDLY *obese* AND DEPRESSED.

All my life I have laughed. I love laughing. As a kid I spent my break times and lunch times roaring laughing around the school yard. When we were younger, we were all altar servers at mass. I broke my mother's heart when I served at Mass. I spent more Sundays with my head bent down trying my hardest not to roar laughing. Once my friend's ring got caught on the bell and I honestly thought I was going to topple off the altar. With my mother's eyes burning into the back of me I practically crawled off the altar and into the sacristy to get myself together. Genuinely laughing has always been my favourite thing.

It's such a cliché but by the end of my battle it was the tears of a clown. Slowly and eerily darkness crept in. I was always happy. Yes, I had my down days like any other human but I was always able to snap out of it and have the craic. I don't know when the switch happened exactly but before I knew it, I had opened the door to depression and it was after making itself at home. Depression came to me in many ways. It was spending my days in bed. It was not showering. It was avoiding social situations. It was wanting to not wake up. I would sleep all day on Sunday and that evening order a big takeaway and go back into a deep sleep. I would then spend the night awake and nearly crawling the walls with sadness and stress.

I became very good at social isolation. I was a pro at making up reasons why I couldn't go for coffee with my friends. It was easier to be alone and miserable with only my demons to keep me company. Being sad is exhausting. I couldn't snap out of it this time. It was everywhere. A dark cloud was shadowing my mind and I could see no light at the end of the tunnel. I didn't laugh anymore. I didn't smile anymore. I didn't even want to be around my loved ones as I sadly resented them. I became bitter. I got angry at God and I cursed him for giving me the raw deal. I wished I was born sixth or eighth instead of seventh so I could be happy. I hated myself for being fat.

My mental health was poisoned. I lay in bed on my days off thinking about how disgusting I was. I used to often daydream about waking up one day and I was thin. I was fit. I would be pretty. I dreamt that I would be happy, that I would marry a handsome man and have loads of babies. I would search Facebook looking for nights out and happy memories and I would daydream that it would come back. Sadly, towards the end my daydreams became more sinister and dark. Whenever things got very bad and thoughts of ending my pain by taking my own life entered my head I would think of my mam, my sisters, my nieces and nephews and I would get rid of the thought from my mind. The nights would haunt me. It was like all my demons got louder. I would lay there and as they screamed at me tears dripped onto the pillow. One particular night I frightened myself. I could see no end. I knew that weight was going to kill me. I had nothing left. Weight had stolen my happiness, it had stolen my period, it had stolen my hope for children and love, it had stolen my looks, it had stolen my smile.

One night I Googled how to kill myself. A number popped up for the Samaritans. Without thinking I pressed dial and an older man answered. He was softly spoken and he asked me how I was. I remember saying nothing, I was just crying. His soft voice filled my ear and he told me that he was here and he was listening and that if I didn't want to talk it didn't matter, he was going to stay on the line. He reassured me that it was confidential and that he didn't even want to know my name. He told me that when I was ready to speak, he would listen. I was sitting up in my bed in a dark room and I was scared of what I was going to finally say out loud. After a few minutes I told him that I was scared. I told him that I wanted to die but I didn't want to hurt my family. He simply let me talk. He didn't interrupt me, he just listened to my pain. He talked to me for over an hour and he made me see that I was loved, he helped me see that there were other options. By letting me talk he helped me see sense. I never got his name, I never found out who he was but I am so grateful for him that night. Writing this even now is painful. I am so sad for old Trisha and what she made herself go through.

I can confidently say that 2017 was the worst year of my life. Depression had hit and I was beginning to see no way out for the future. I had lost friends, I cried more than I had laughed and I hated every single part of me. I had lost the ability to hide my pain from loved ones and I wallowed in misery at every moment. I had avoided all social occasions that year. I barely showered.

That Christmas was a tough one. I had spent the whole month of December in constant pain at work. Every single opportunity I got, I had to sit down. I couldn't bend down anymore and I was in everyone's way, including my own. I didn't buy any new clothes for Christmas Day like I had done every year. I had just gone to Evans on Christmas Eve and picked up some Christmas pyjamas that were size 30.

As the sores under my stomach bled, I packed them with napkins to stop the chafing; as my knees screamed in pain my heart broke into pieces. I knew that I couldn't get away with this anymore. I drove home that evening with the sound of my sobs filling the car, terrified it would be my last Christmas.

The next day I did my usual and I started to make the dinner. I didn't drink because I knew there was no point. I knew I couldn't get out of my own head enough to have fun and I knew it would make me very down when I was left alone. It was the first year I didn't care what was under the tree for me. I knew not one thing was going to make me happy. I spent the day filled with negative thoughts and thinking how much easier it would be for my family if I wasn't here. This is so sad for me to remember because with the size of my family Christmas Day is like something from the Wild West. The house is filled with fun, laughter, love and loads of competitive games. We argue when someone takes our seat, we drink wine, we fill our bellies with delicious turkey and we always get sad on Christmas night as it's another year over. Christmas is a happy time for us.

That Christmas my sister Maura had three-month-old twins – my gorgeous nephews. For some reason the naps didn't work out so she missed dinner with us. We decided that we would drop down their dinners and once the boys were awake, they could come up home and join us for the Christmas festivities. I wrapped their dinners up and Annie and I headed to Dad's car to drop them down. Maura lives about a two-minute walk from my house but I couldn't even walk that far at this stage. Annie hopped into the passenger seat and I had to reverse Dad's car out of the gate. I couldn't do it – my stomach was jammed into the steering wheel and I couldn't turn it. As I burned with embarrassment Annie came around to my side and tugged me from the car. By the time I stood up I knew I had been found out. I begged her not to tell the girls – I was so ashamed. She assured me she wouldn't. Afterwards I found out that she cried herself to sleep and it totally ruined her Christmas. I spent the rest of that Christmas Day avoiding Annie. My stomach was in so much pain, I just wanted to go into bed and be left alone. I couldn't play with my nephews and nieces. I could do nothing only feel sad.

A few weeks passed and one Sunday Annie asked me to join her for a pregnancy scan. We drove to Cork and sat in the waiting room of CUMH. I was riddled with anxiety that someone would ask me when I was due so I went in and out for cigarettes, I went to the shop about a hundred times to avoid anyone speaking to me. As we sat chatting about random stuff, Annie brought up a fitness page that she had seen. She had told me that she was going to do it after the baby was born.

I could see through her. I knew it was her way to try and push me towards exercise without hurting me. The chairs in the waiting room had a lever in between them and I had to lift it up as it was tearing into my sides. I was the biggest woman in the maternity hospital.

When the midwife called her name I automatically stood up. I was like, there is no way that I have waited for hours with you and I don't get to see the scan. It was the best move of my life. I didn't know it at the time but when I was walking into see a scan I was also walking into my future. I've never had children so I've only seen a sonogram on television and it was so exciting. I stood back as the midwife popped the jelly on Annie's belly and all I could hear was the gentle purr of the machine and the nurses outside. Within seconds a sound echoed in my ears. A heartbeat. That's the moment my world came crumbling down. I stepped back. My bond, my unconditional love that I have for each and every one of my nieces and nephews is something I'm proud of. I will always be the fun aunt. I will always be the bold aunt. I will always be the one that drives them bonkers and leaves them to their parents then. I will always be the one that will act the ape. So, as this heartbeat filled the room, I felt that I wouldn't know this child. My chest tightened as I realised that I would either be dead or in a home. This baby would never know his aunt like all his cousins did. In all honesty that moment was the scariest moment of my life. I will never forget the cold sense of dread that crept over me.

When Annie came out of the room, she marched towards me and told me to sit down and listen. She told me that she was scared. She told me that all the girls were frightened and sick with worry. She told me she was terrified her baby sister was going to die, she couldn't watch it anymore. She told me that her baby needed their mad aunt. She begged me to promise her I would at least try. That was all she wanted, she told me that they all believed in me. As I listened, tears spilled down my face. I told her everything. I told her how scared I was. I explained that I didn't want to die, I told her I was sorry for everything and that I needed help. She explained to me how they had countless chats about how to help me. She told me I wasn't alone and they would all help me fix it. We decided there and then that we would buy the online diet that she had shown me earlier. We got a lovely nurse on reception to download the questionnaire and I paid the €200 via PayPal and hope finally surfaced. The best thing about this lightbulb moment is that once we left the hospital it was late and we were starving so we got some McDonalds. That's what I mean by the lightbulb moment only lasting a second, but once you have access to the house, don't go back out, stay in there.

The next day I did what I usually did and buried my head in the sand. I ignored Annie's texts and I blocked her out. I knew that the online diet that was sent to me was never going to work. It was not sustainable and was a simple copy and paste job. It's tough being obese but when your suggested exercises are pull ups it's even tougher!

Fast forward two weeks later: 5 February 2018. I was lying in bed miserable and in and out of a tortured sleep. I was back living at home as I was struggling on my own. My phone beeped beside me and it was a text from Annie stating that it was the first Monday of the month; is there any way I would try and make this my month? My immediate emotion was rage. How dare she text me this? Did she not know the pain I was in? She hadn't a clue what pain was like. I texted her back and I told her no. I told her to get lost. I was a failure. I couldn't do it. I was turning 30 the following month and all I had done over the years was get fatter. I told her to move on and forget about me. I had messed my whole life up. That right there was another lightbulb moment – and the light was slowly getting brighter. I had finally admitted to myself that it was me who was giving up. **I finally stopped blaming everyone else and took ownership of myself.**

That text message was *the start of my life.*

Me and Mr Dan Sweeney, my best friend.
He has been a rock to me on my journey.

I threw the phone down and my throat tightened and tears spilled from my eyes. I had failed yet again. As I lay there panic set in. I had realised I was giving up. I lay there and I was fit to punch someone or burst into tears. My emotions were high and my energy was low. I lay there in my unwashed sheets and I cried. As I cried, I replayed what I had sent Annie. I was so confused. My head was telling me give up but my heart was yelling the opposite. I remember talking to myself. I remember asking myself angrily if this was it. Was I finished? I didn't want this to be the end. I didn't want to give up. I wanted to live.

Starting the gym

To this day I don't know where the strength came from but I pulled myself out of the bed. I sat at the edge of the bed unwashed, tired, panting and lightheaded like I did most mornings after trying to get up. I pulled on a black top, black pants and a green cardigan. I shoved my feet into old socks and worn Skechers and I grabbed my handbag. I didn't know exactly what I was doing but it was something. I met my Mam in the kitchen, I told her I was off to Cork and that I loved her loads. Afterwards Mam told me she felt something was different that morning. I had pulled the curtains and opened the top windows on the way down the hall, which I never did as I was so depressed. She said as I walked out the door she hoped and prayed I was on the way to the gym. The guilt I feel for the worry I gave my mother is intense. I'll never be able to repay her for minding me like a true mother when things got tough for me as an adult. Thankfully her gut was right.

I flung myself into my car and I picked up my phone. I sent a Facebook message to an old trainer and asked him was he around. When I didn't get a reply I called a gym in Cork. I explained to the woman on the phone that I had a lot of weight to lose and she didn't even hesitate and explained the packages to me. I made the journey to Cork and it was awful. I spent every single second convincing myself to turn back, to just book the gastric bypass again and just cop on as the gym wasn't the place for me. I couldn't have been more wrong.

In the meantime, my sister Annie had texted me and was taking none of my dramatics. She sent me a picture of a baby lamb running through a field and she told me to cop on – that this lamb was me. She told me that I would fix it all and all the family adored me.

As I pulled into the car park I was on auto pilot and I walked into the gym. I had cash on me and it felt like a scene from *Pretty Woman* when Julia Roberts has all this money – could someone help her? I stood at the counter and started the paperwork for joining the gym. It was a Monday so the lady behind the counter told me that we would start on the Monday of the next week. My heart sank and with a trembling lip I told her that I couldn't walk back out the door as I wasn't sure I would come back again. She sensed my fear and told me to wait a moment. My green cardigan had a huge rip under the armpit which is another sign of how much I didn't care about how I looked. A woman who was queueing behind me touched my bare arm and pointed out kindly that I had a rip in my jumper. The feeling of someone's touch on my unwashed skin made me feel sick and I snapped at her to not touch me. When the lady came back, she told me that she could fit me in with a woman called Emma the following morning at 11.30 a.m. I thanked her and left. When I was in the car, I sat there for ages thinking about what I had just done. I picked the phone up and I called my sister Annie. As we chatted, I told her I had joined the gym. She was so confused as she thought I was still in bed being dramatic and sad. I asked her not to tell Mam or the girls and if I was to fail at least no one else would know. She promised me she wouldn't.

That night I announced it to our sister WhatsApp group. Secrets are not my thing! I asked them to say nothing and ask no questions. I was sick of failing and scared of building it up too much only to upset them again.

I had no gym clothes that fitted me. I had no sports bra. I could not wear underwear as my stomach kept making it roll down, I had no range of motion and I was so deeply depressed. I went into Debenhams, picked up a pair of John Rocha black stretchy pyjamas and wore them as gym

Practising box jumps in the gym.

pants for the first few weeks. The next day, as I was driving up the road to Cork, I realised in a huge panic I was going to run out of petrol. The most Trisha thing to happen on the biggest day of my life. I was so mad at myself. I was shouting and roaring at myself in the car calling myself an eejit and that I had once again messed it all up. The drama was unnecessary, and I think my subconscious was trying to find a way to give up but **thankfully my dream was already bigger than my fears.**

I was so scared that I was too big for the gym. That the machines wouldn't even take my weight. When I went into the consultation room, I knew I smelled, I know how awful I looked, and I knew I was morbidly obese. I truly didn't care at that point. I knew I was at the point of no return and if this didn't work, I wouldn't survive. When Emma weighed me, I was so paranoid that my feet smelled. As I heard the words, you are 26 stone, I didn't even flinch. I didn't care. She then took my measurements and I was so ashamed as the tape didn't go around certain parts. I felt so awkward as she struggled to get measurements. I remember when she said we would take some photos. I wanted the ground to swallow me. I couldn't make eye contact with the camera and I wished over and over again that I was anywhere but there. The feeling of gratefulness for having those photos will always stay with me. **If you are reading this and you're too scared of taking the photo, just do it. It will become your 'before' photo and you will look back on it with such pride.** So that concluded the consultation and I made my way to the private studio where me and Emma embarked on the scariest and most wonderful journey.

Emma became a great friend. She said that she would look after me three times a week for 30 minutes and that I had to leave all my baggage at the door and just work my ass off in the gym. If anyone tells you the first few weeks are easy, please do not believe them. You are panicking that this personal trainer who you don't know is judging you because you don't know how to squat. I hated every single second of that first day in that gym. Quickly Emma learned that I had a phobia of mirrors so she made sure I was never facing one when I worked out. I was so ashamed at how immobile I had become – I had to hold onto a chair to attempt a lunge forward. The whole session my eyes burned with tears and all I wanted to do was pick a fight with Emma and storm out of the gym but something held me there. **I knew that if I left, I was finished.**

Baby weights and tears

A few days in I still absolutely hated every second of it, I was literally crying and telling Emma I couldn't do it, I couldn't even lift a small weight. I kept repeating how useless I was, then Emma told me to stop. She told me that I was so inside my head that I was not allowing myself to do anything. I will never forget the line she said to me, 'If I told you to lift a car you couldn't, but if a car fell on someone you loved sheer adrenaline would help you lift it. It is mind over matter.' It sounds mad but for two solid months I repeated over and over in my head, 'If a car fell on Mam, I would lift it,' and things slowly started to get easier. It was another step in the right direction and out of my own way. **I went from barely able to lift my arm above my head to knowing what a deadlift and a hack squat is.**

The next three months of training went by and I spent most of my sessions silently attacking myself, paranoid that my trainer was judging me. My body was racked with aches and pains, screaming at me to go back to normal, telling me I wasn't able, telling me to give up. It was all in my head. No one judged me in the gym.

The trainer does not care if you can't squat – they are there to help you, so

don't ever worry about being judged.

My promise to the bump

When this was going on my sister Annie and I had another big chat. She told me that the baby she was expecting needed their Aunt Trisha, that she needed her sister to be there for her when she had her first child. I made a promise to her bump to try very hard. I spent every day connecting with a baby that I didn't know. When my legs ached, I thought of this person growing in my sister's belly and how much they meant to me. In June 2018 the most wonderful little man entered my world. Danny. When I met him at the hospital I stared at his gorgeous little face. He had finally arrived, my little hero. On his Babygro were the words, 'Trisha, will you be my godmother? Love Danny'. I cried like a baby. Danny's new life gave me my new life. I was sinking and he became my life jacket. He knew I was struggling without even knowing me. I will always show him that comfort zones are there to be pushed and I will forever be grateful for him.

Now I have gone from feeling like I was so out of place to feeling like I'm the queen of the gym. I have gone from not looking into the mirror for the first three months to using the mirror to watch my technique. I have gone from wearing pyjamas to wearing the brightest-coloured leggings in the gym. My laughter is back and I never take that for granted. Being able to laugh so hard my back aches is one of my favourite parts of this mad journey I am on. The relief to find myself smiling and meaning it is insane. I will never let things get as bad as I did in the past. I will never let something take my smile again. So now as I look in the mirror and I see myself looking back I don't mock myself; I don't cringe. I smile and tell myself I'm a hero, I'm beautiful, I am enough. **Don't let the black dog win. Grab it by the scruff of the neck and fire it out the window.** You can fix it. The tears will stop. You can take back your life.

The first Instagram post!

The reason why you are reading this book at all is because on one mad Monday evening I decided that in the most public way possible I would document my journey on Instagram. I was 24 stone and for the first time in quite a while a strange feeling had come over me. I can identify that now as pride. Although the first few weeks in the gym were awful, I knew it was my last chance. I had no backup plan – it was this or death or a stroke. So, each day that I turned up I decided that it was another day for me to save my life.

It's ironic that after weeks avoiding the mirrors in the gym I turned to Emma one day and asked her to record a set for me. It was so out of the blue that I don't think either of us registered what we were doing. Afterwards I didn't look at the video, I just went home. I sat in the car outside and contemplated what I was going to do with it. I decided to send it to Colin. Colin is my buddy in Australia who would have always encouraged me to lose weight through sheer brutal honesty and it always came from such a good place. I had cut him off for about two years as I wasn't mentally able for his encouraging words. In the video I am wearing a top from Penneys, a pair of jeggings from Evans and runners. I am facing away from the mirror and I am not looking directly at the camera. From Brisbane Colin replied that he was so proud of me, he had a tear in his eye watching me work out and I was adorable, but my runners were disgusting and to cop on.

He was so right and it's typical of our friendship to not hold back. He told me that I should put the video on Instagram and show people what I was doing, that it was so motivating. I was horrified and terrified that he would put it on Facebook and tag me so I replied and said that I would

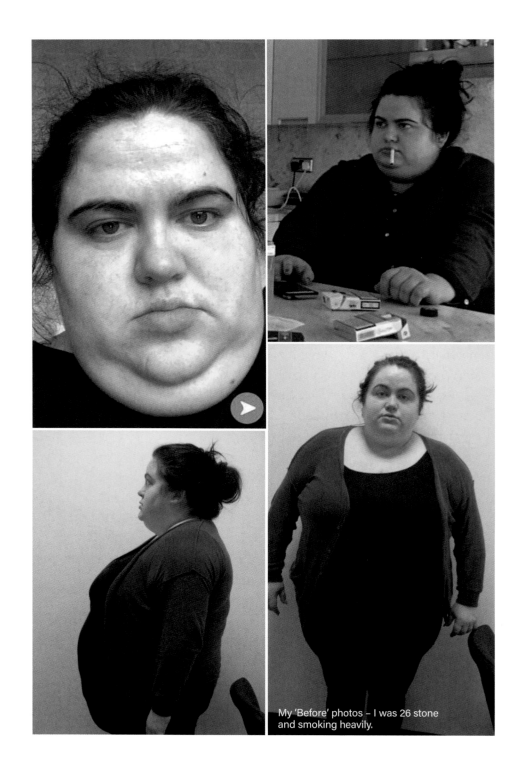

My 'Before' photos – I was 26 stone and smoking heavily.

wait until I had all the weight lost and then I would show people how I did it. I told him that I didn't want people to see how big I was, I would have been mortified. To this Colin simply replied, **'Trisha get over yourself – people know how fat you are; you could help someone.'** Colin, I love you for being the most honest friend I have. Thank you for the push!

That evening I was sitting on the couch with Mam after texting Colin, showing her some videos of my workouts. She was so chuffed and was praising me and exclaiming how small I looked and how much weight I had lost. I decided then that I was going to set up an Instagram page. Ironically, I didn't want to do it on Facebook because too many people who would have known me would have seen it and I was shy. I was texting my friend Laura and I had my name organised and was ready to rock. I was going to name my page 'Trisha's-trek-to-trim'. I remember she messaged me back instantly and was like, please do not do that. It's too long, it's weird, and we went back and forth for ages until eventually she was like, why don't you keep it simple and call it 'Trisha's transformation'. I remember scoffing, thinking that it was too simple. Thankfully I listened. Pressing 'post' for the first time was terrifying.

After the first day I had 400 followers and I was blown away. I was shocked to the core. I texted my sister Kellie and I was like, can you imagine if I had 1000 followers by Christmas. That Christmas I had 17,000 amazing transformers. Every day my page grew and grew and messages of support poured in. It started to become a vital piece of my journey and my healing. I decided from day one that I would keep my page true to me and what I feel. I decided that my stories would be my workout videos and a bit of craic and my grid would be serious chats about my lifestyle. I didn't hold back and told the truth. Transformers came from all across the country and the world. It was the most surreal feeling in the world. Slowly my confidence started to build. **I started to see what my transformers were telling me.** I could see an inspiration, I could see a lovely girl, I could see a hero.

A dream come true: *The Late Late Show*

As my confidence grew, I became cocky and on a Friday night in September 2018 I came home and my mam and my aunt Nora were sitting at the table watching *The Late Late Show*. I declared that someday I would sit on that brown couch and would tell my story. They looked knowingly at each other and Mam said, 'Well I believe you, Trisha, you will get there.' That January I was at my sister Annie's house recording a live video for Instagram and I got a random Facebook message from a producer for *The Late Late Show* asking me to appear on the show. I genuinely thought it was a joke. I ran at Annie and nearly picked her up and threw her at the wall with joy. I'll never ever forget the joy I felt at that moment. Trisha Lewis was going on *The Late Late Show*.

My dream was coming true. On the Thursday I arrived in Dublin floating on a cloud. The messages were pouring into my phone and people were cheering me on from all around the country. I couldn't sleep that night, my stomach was doing flips. My sister Juliette flew in from London and we met by the Spire and spun each other around in euphoria. She was so proud of me. We all had a family dinner in the hotel before the show – me, my mam, Kellie, Juliette, Annie and Michelle. I was so scared and nervous. I cannot describe how delirious I felt when I landed in RTÉ. I sat in the green room and Ryan made his way directly to my table while searching for the woman of the moment, the star of the show. As I stood up to shake his hand I stumbled and my first words were, 'Jesus, Ryan, I am falling for you.' Like, cringe! Thankfully he roared laughing and the ice was broken.

Ryan sat across from me and he asked me how I was feeling. He then went on to tell me not to worry, this was just a chat between Ryan and Trisha, forget the audience, forget the cameras. He told me that I was a hero, that the whole of Ireland was rooting for me. He told me that he would never shame me, or mock me, he just wanted to talk to Trisha. It took all my fears away and I told him that I was ready. After that it became fun. I got a picture with him while my sister nearly knocked him to the ground trying to get her picture with him. He got a fright as she literally tackled him from the side. Michelle makes me laugh so much, she is so unique and so supportive, and she was backstage in her element with Mary Black. Ryan gave me a huge hug and I asked him to meet me at the end of the three steps in case I fell. We laughed and I told him if I was going down, he was too. I asked him could I just be filmed as much as possible from my shoulders up. He said no problem and asked me why? I told him that I was conscious of my side profile and my belly. His exact words were, 'Trisha, that is your USP, that is you and that's what makes you beautiful. Own it.' I have never once since that moment hated my stomach, I now own it and wear it with pride while knowing it's on the way out. As I heard the band start playing, I was backstage, the girl who'd cried herself to sleep, the girl who'd rung the Samaritans, the girl who'd hated herself. I was being miked up and someone was powdering my face. I was wearing my jumpsuit from Dunnes because I was conscious I couldn't cross my legs because of my stomach so my designer dress was left at home. I didn't want to go *Basic Instinct* on *The Late Late*! How had this happened me? Ryan popped his head around the curtain and with the biggest smile told me I was going to be amazing.

Then I heard my intro, heard the song 'Change Your Life' being belted out by the band and I quickly hugged my sister and with 17,000 followers and a beating heart I stepped out onto the biggest show on Irish television. True to his word Ryan was waiting for me at the steps and gave me a huge hug. I sat down and I told Ireland my story. I told Ireland my pain, my joy, I made jokes, I laughed with Ryan, I waved at my mam, I told all of Ireland I was single and I had fun. I spoke with honesty, I didn't care. I was here speaking for old Trisha, this was the moment I needed. Ryan treated me with respect, he showed me empathy and he made me feel safe. I knew he would never mock me so I told my story in the most honest way possible. Before I knew it sadly the interview was over, but as Ryan wrapped it up the most beautiful thing happened. People in the audience started to stand up, to cheer and roar, to clap loudly. I was getting a STANDING OVATION. Ryan told me to look and to enjoy it – I deserved it. Instead of absorbing it all I started to roar and shout in typical Trisha form, 'They are creating a monster!' I have never felt that feeling ever and I will forever be grateful to the audience members that night. As the ad break started the audience roared and whistled at me and I met my sister who was waiting for me with tears of pride in her eyes. Ryan made his way up to Mam, shook her hand and asked her how proud she was. Michelle excitedly told me that while I sat on the couch I had gained 12,000 new eyes on my page and the messages were overwhelming.

For the next few days people from all over the country sent me thousands of messages and my following keeps growing. People are not cruel as I once thought.

My transformers are kind and sweet and they are rooting for me.

Rooting for me to beat the bulge.

Life after *The Late Late*: keeping up momentum

O ver the next few months I made sure that the gym, water and food were my priority. I didn't look ahead at the 13 stone that I still had to lose. I only looked at it pound by pound. Sometimes the pounds went; other times they missed me too much so they came back on. I started to celebrate the small wins like wearing a different colour top, being able to pick up a biro from the floor without getting dizzy or being able to wear shoes with laces. No win was too small.

On the night of the *The Late Late Show* I realised that my weight was my USP for the moment and from the very next day I truly accepted myself and fell in love. The hardest curveball that I came across was the closure of my gym which meant I lost my personal trainer Emma, who had been so important in starting me on this journey. The rug was pulled from under me and I was so scared. My weight was plateauing and the scales kept giving the same reading, so I took my own advice and I got up and fixed it. I had to find a gym that suited me – I was with NRG Health and Fitness and trained with Will, who is an amazing guy and a good friend of mine, but the commute just didn't suit me. Once again, I had to put myself first, so now I train in FlyeFit with Jamie. Let me tell you, the DOMS are well and truly back!

Since *The Late Late Show* I have achieved the following:

- I can now do a sit up.
- I can plank.
- I can do higher box jumps.
- I have started running.

If your gym routine isn't working for you, my advice would be to change it up. You can move – you are not a tree! Just make sure that the change you make is benefiting your fitness, not an excuse to avoid challenging yourself.

Making friends at 31 seems difficult in theory. To me it became the easiest thing in the world. Once I started to love myself it became easier to let others love me. I've been able to share my story with so many amazing people. I became brand ambassador for *The Echo* Mini Marathon, I set up a running club with Dan Sweeney called Street Crew where a community gathers twice a week for running with the most important thing: no judgement. I went to Kathryn Thomas's bootcamp. I arrived alone, but after spending a few days with like-minded people I found that it was so much fun. I have made more friends than I ever thought was possible and am having so much craic. I set a podcast up with Dan called *The Trisha and Dan Show* where we pop on for the chats and the laughs once a week. Brian Keane and Paul Dermody are a constant online support and are always on hand for advice and a bit of craic. I made friends with Marty Guilfoyle and when we are together, I feel like I am 10 again. The first time I met him was in a gym after I had tried to cancel on him loads and he wasn't having any of it. I am so glad he is now in my life. I have stopped assuming people won't like me or judge me. I went hiking in Dublin with Dan and Shane – totally out of my comfort zone. Shane is another vital part of my new circle of friends. Before we left for our hike, I nearly got sick I was so scared, was riddled in anxiety that I wasn't able. Dan and Shane simply said, 'If it takes you seven hours that is seven hours we spend with Trisha, that's all that matters to us. It doesn't matter how long it takes you we are here with you.' I danced the night away with the two of them in Copper Face Jacks, which is huge for me as I avoided nightclubs for years and years; to feel so happy and comfortable in a club was amazing. Life is surreal at the moment.

I had to deal with a few trolls online and my baby sister moved to Melbourne with the amazing Kev Cronin. I miss them terribly but I cannot wait to hop off the plane in Melbourne as healthy as can be. **I won't have to worry anymore about the seatbelt extension because for the first time, the seatbelt on the plane fits me!**

I am in the middle of my weight loss journey. I have 8 stone gone and my day-one dream was to lose 13 stone 1 lb which is just over half my body weight. I am looking forward to being able to cross my legs, I am excited about being able to comfortably tie a buckle on a boot without my stomach being in the way, I am excited about wearing proper underwear that doesn't fall down because my belly is in the way and they slip. I am looking forward to someday having children of my own – opportunities I thought I had lost in my darkest times are back again. My period came back with a bang and now I am delighted and so grateful for it! Most of all I am excited for life. I have a long way to go but mentally I am home. Mentally I feel safe and happy and I am no longer scared, I know that if I keep on going, I will get there.

I will lead the way for anyone suffering out there and I will show them that it can and will be done, I will continue on with my army of a family and

I will continue on beating the bulge.

if I can
DO IT
YOU CAN
TOO

My precious transformers, let me tell you something: if I can do this, anyone can. I was you reading this and, in some cases, worse. You have one piece of information that I didn't have. You are a transformer and you are reading this book in the hope that it will help you too. It will if you just step out of your own way. Take the bull by the horns and go put on some runners, make a plan, execute it and be the CEO of your own world.

How to get started

Find your why

Your why needs to be bigger than you. My why was the bump and that is what kept me going for the first few months.

Meet your demons

Meeting my demons was an important part of my journey. Once you can see them and identify them, they are smaller in real life. Once you tell them who is boss, they listen. They'll never go but you can learn how to control them and eventually become friends with them. You can learn from what they say and prove them wrong.

Often when I overate, I would be riddled with guilt and shame. I would be filled with rage as my stomach would be so full it hurt and the only thing that would help would be a nap. I would bottle it up and give my demons more power.

The amount of times I have dined alone in a restaurant on a Sunday and ordered a starter before my starter – I have lost count. I would always have a sense of panic and order way too much and would be so embarrassed when I was in company. I would justify the amount that I ordered by paying the bill and that would be it. My friend Michelle said that it used to break her heart if we got a takeaway and I would always make sure that I paid and called in the order. I would lay out the food in the kitchen and bring it to her in the sitting room. When I was in the kitchen, I would eat the extra food that I had secretly ordered for myself. I would secretly eat to fill the void that was so overwhelming it would make me dizzy. Loneliness. I was never addicted to the amount of food that I was eating; I was addicted to the disgusting feeling. After eating so much my stomach would be in pain, I would be sweating, drowsy and sad. I was reaffirming my inner demons that I was in fact the horrible person I told myself I was.

About five months in to my transformation I was training with Emma and was all over the place. I was riddled in guilt. I was holding a secret from her and I was terrified she would cop it. She eventually asked me what was wrong as I was being a total weirdo and I told her that I had messed up the previous Sunday and I felt rotten over it. I went on to explain that I had eaten four Snickers ice-creams. She told me to relax, it was okay, I was human and that most humans have done that when they buy a multipack, they eat them all, the temptation was too much for me and that I shouldn't buy the box anymore.

After a few minutes I was like, 'Emma, I need to tell you something else. It wasn't a multipack.' She looked at me, confused. I told her I'd stopped at the Maxol shop and bought one ice-cream and drove the 15 minutes home after inhaling it. As I sat at home, I started to feel regret that I'd rushed eating it so back I got into the car to buy another one – this one I would savour and enjoy. About two hours later, sitting at home, I started to think more about how really lovely those ice-creams were and in my head convinced myself a third one would make no difference – I had eaten too much anyway. So into the car I hopped and made my way back to the shop and picked up the third ice-cream. After eating it at the petrol station I drove out the road but in true Trisha style I turned the car around after three minutes, pulled in, got another ice-cream and well and truly drove the nail into the calorie-deficit coffin that day!

As I relayed my story, I think Emma was secretly horrified and proud at how well I executed the plan. To this day it makes me smile at how crazy

Me and Kathryn Thomas having so much fun at her Pure Results bootcamp.

and irrational I became at the simple taste of ice-cream. The truth is I admitted this and no one really cared. Some people have found it gas, others have been bemused but no one truly cares. I publicly spoke about it on the Brian Keane podcast and the floods of messages from people relating or in general thinking it was hilarious was so brilliant. **I wasn't the monster that my demons had told me I was. I was just an eejit that had no self-control around a Snickers ice-cream.**

Everyone has these demons – the voices that tell you that you're not good enough, that you're a monster. The first step is to meet them and recognise that they are not as powerful as you think.

Take the power away from your demons

When I joined the gym, I had to argue with myself to keep going, I had to silence the voice in my head telling me I wasn't good enough, I had to wrestle my inner demons so much. I was just starting a mad adventure but I had to feel the low so I could compare it to the high that I am feeling now.

I spent the first two months training in a studio downstairs as I was too afraid of being seen upstairs in the main gym, petrified that I would become a meme and people would laugh at my size. One day I walked in and I met Emma and said, 'Let's go upstairs' – I gave her no warning and off up we went. I was crippled in anxiety and I wanted to cry, but when I walked into the main gym not one person looked at me, no one stared, no one honestly cared – every single person in the gym is there for themselves.

A few weeks in I was walking down the stairs and three men were coming against me. As we passed each other one guy said, 'Congratulations on all your hard work.' I quickly thanked him and glanced back, expecting them to be laughing at me in a huddle but they weren't, they were just walking on. I had given the gym such a bad image in my head and demonised it when in fact the gym was the safest place for me. **My dream is that every single person with weight loses the irrational fear that the gym is only for fit people. It is for every single person in the world.**

You can learn to stop reaffirming your demons. You can learn to step out of your own way and give yourself a chance, to look for help and to look back with pride on how far you have come.

Reset and move on

When you are just about to overindulge and you know how crap you feel afterwards, simply tell yourself to own it, decide that you will not feel bad, reset and move on. There's no point in feeding yourself lies to justify things, you are the only person with the power to fix it. Once you form this healthier relationship with food, over time the urge to overindulge does become less and less. It becomes less sinister and less of a dirty secret, so the appeal goes. You will not let the word 'guilt' surround your meals or your nights out.

You will reset and you will beat the bulge.

I have always separated food into evil and good but the fact about it is food is incredible; as a chef my career is to look at food with love, respect and imagination. I started to enjoy meals out with family and friends and realised that this was living and we were creating memories. We shouldn't demonise the fact that we had some cake. I quickly realised that I was in control now and I wasn't letting my emotions win.

I also realised that buying the multipack is never ever a good idea. You will end up eating more than you should and you will have guilt. So, I decided that multipacks were now banned and I would just purchase the one item if I was going to have some ice-cream or chocolate.

Me in Spain, living
my best life.

How to keep going

Stop comparing yourself to others

When 'motivation' is looked up on the internet the following description comes up:

'Motivation is the word derived from the word "motive" which means, desires, want or drive within the individual. It is the process of stimulating people to actions to accomplish the goals.'

I read this and it makes me laugh. Motivation and weight loss should never be used in the same bracket. The simple fact is that motivation does not exist. I feel it is an unfair item to sell to people who are struggling. When you start searching for motivation the sad fact is you become bitterly disappointed. You go down the scary road of comparisons and wondering why you aren't as motivated as Mary down the road. Why can't you go to the gym like everyone on Instagram? Why do your feet feel like they are stuck in cement at the simple thought of going outside for a walk?

Ditch the motivation myth

It's because you are focusing on the wrong word. **The words that you should focus on are habit, discipline, self-love and hard work.** When you pick up a box of cigarettes you create a habit. You open the wrapper, you pop the cigarette into your mouth, you reach for your lighter, you spark up, you inhale and you exhale and you repeat. You keep going so you smoke every single time you feel the need or the desire to. That structure didn't come from motivation, it came from habit. Once this was pointed out to me it all made sense. Everything I had read, everything I had assumed about fit, healthy people was all a figment of my imagination. Motivation didn't and had never existed. Habits were formed by these people and just like when I used to smoke, they had the determination to keep going. They have the discipline to go to the gym just like I always had the discipline to go to the shop to buy fags. They work hard just like I worked hard to buy cigarettes.

Stick to a realistic set of rules

So just like that I discarded the word 'motivation' and I try and live by a small set of rules that I visit each day. Without fail on a Sunday I will head to Aldi and get in my weekly shop. If I do not do this (in general) my week is going to go wrong. Temptation will pop its head up. I make sure that I do not buy too many treats as the reality of it is, I will eat them in one sitting and not ration them out.

I make sure that I never miss my gym session or never put off a walk that I had told myself I would do. The fact is it isn't worth it and you're only fooling yourself. Skipping your gym session is silly. No matter how much you want to cancel or not go, just go, you will never ever regret a session. No matter how much you feel like you are too tired or you're not in the mood or it's too rainy, do not give in. **The times you really don't want to go are the times that you need to go.**

Be selfish and learn to say 'no'

At the beginning of my weight loss I had decided that my 'why' had to be bigger than my 'how'. I had to want this more than anything I had ever wanted. I made a decision that for the first time in my life I was going to become selfish and put myself completely first. Weight loss was now going to become as important as breathing. I would have always been the first person to jump in and help someone before I helped myself. I would cancel a gym session or a walk so I could lend a hand. It became easier to be someone else's hero than my own. So, on day one I started to retrain everything I had practised in the past, I started to say the simple word 'no' more often if I felt that it wouldn't be beneficial to me or my weight loss journey.

Take it step by step

My end goal of weight loss was the only focus I had for the first few months. I started to take it step by step and that is such a cliché but literally each step I took, I thought about it. I set about tasks every second. My first task is straight into the shower. I then go to the kitchen, pop on the kettle and make my breakfast. I organise my food that I will be having that day by either cooking it or taking it from the batch-cooked items I've stored in the fridge. I fill my water bottle and I promise myself that I will smash today. Along the way if I slip up I try my hardest to reset immediately. **One bad meal will not make you fat; neither will one good meal make you thin.** Consistency is key. I have the habit of giving up if I eat something I shouldn't have at lunch and I tell myself the lie that I will reset tomorrow, when the best possible thing you can do is to reset immediately. If you are walking down the street and you end up tripping you don't lay down and prepare to die, do you? You get right back up immediately, dust yourself off and continue on with your day. If you use this mentality for your weight loss it becomes easier to reset.

Enjoy the journey

At the start of this whole regime I made a vow that I would enjoy the journey so I could be happy at my destination. There is no point taking on the challenge as something of a negative. Look at the weight you have to lose and smile. This is now your 'why'. This is now your Everest. This is the reason you will get out of bed each morning and this will be your purpose. I see every single day as a challenge, I look at the gym and exercise not only as weight loss tools but as a sport. You do not have to look a certain way to become an athlete. **You do not have to be thin to enjoy the gym.**

Getting the train up from Mallow for *The Late Late Show!*

WHAT you can do RIGHT NOW

I'm giving you the steps and guidelines that I used at the beginning of this journey so that you can follow in my footsteps. Every step is equally important and once they are all married together you will have the perfect recipe for a successful, sustainable weight loss.

1
Ask yourself three questions

I wake up every single morning and I ask
myself three vital questions.

Do I want to be fat or fit?

Do I want to be happy or sad?

Do I want to be healthy or dying?

When I answer these questions,

I rise up.

2
Make a realistic plan

Sit down and see what time you have to change your life. The excuse that you do not have time is not a reason. If you calculate how much time you spend pressing the snooze button or scrolling on your phone you will quickly realise that you have 30 minutes to give yourself a chance of getting rid of whatever pounds are bothering you. If you calculate how much time you spend thinking about your weight you will realise that a 30-minute session is doable.

Identify curveballs

If you have a day that you are travelling and you are out of routine, plan around this. Make sure that your weight loss is just as important on these days as on any other day. Simple things like having your car full of petrol so you are not stopping at the garage and therefore tempted by the sweets at the till can be put into place. At the start of the week identify any curveballs that will come your way and tackle them head on. If you know that you will be tempted, bring some healthy snacks with you in your bag.

Give yourself time

You have to become a bit selfish to succeed. Make some time in your day and week that will facilitate you beating the bulge. You will need to allocate time for your weekly shop, your exercise and your meals.

3
Look at your diet

Tackle the cupboards

Clean up your diet now. Now being the key word. Do not wait for the junk food press to be all eaten as you will waste money. Go to the press, grab the sweets and crisps and dump them.

Write your shopping list

At the start I found this so difficult. I hadn't done a weekly shop in around five years. I had spent my time going from day to day and shop to shop without ever having a rhythm to my diet, which led me to become 26 stone. Make this a part of your week and nothing changes that. The weeks that I skip Aldi and say the age-old lie that I will do it tomorrow are the weeks that I will 100 per cent see a gain on the scales as I have lost control again. Here is a sample of what my weekly shopping list looks like:

Frozen

- [ ] Raspberries
- [ ] Basil
- [ ] Garlic
- [ ] Ginger
- [ ] Peas
- [ ] Sweetcorn

Fruit and vegetables

- [ ] Carrots
- [ ] Spinach
- [ ] Red onions
- [ ] Mushrooms
- [ ] Mandarin oranges
- [ ] Bananas
- [ ] Raspberries
- [ ] Strawberries
- [ ] Tenderstem broccoli
- [ ] Baby potatoes
- [ ] Cherry tomatoes
- [ ] Rocket
- [ ] Iceberg lettuce

Meat and dairy

- [ ] Natural yoghurt
- [ ] Beef medallions
- [ ] Salmon fillets
- [ ] Low-fat milk
- [ ] Cottage cheese
- [ ] Chicken breasts
- [ ] Free range eggs
- [ ] Grated parmesan

Cupboard

- [ ] Cajun spices
- [ ] Soy sauce
- [ ] Meridian 100% peanut butter
- [ ] Wholegrain wraps
- [ ] Oats
- [ ] Sesame oil
- [ ] Sesame seeds
- [ ] Olive oil or low-calorie spray
- [ ] Garlic purée
- [ ] 85% dark chocolate
- [ ] Basmati rice

Create a meal plan

Below I give a sample meal plan to get you started. It may seem like a pain to do this but it really helps to keep you on the right track during a busy week. Some meals are from the book, some aren't, but you'll get the idea!

	Monday	Tuesday	Wednesday
Breakfast	Berry and peanut butter oats Page 96	Savoury omelette Page 130	Berry and peanut butter oats Page 96
Lunch	Couscous Page 206	Swede, coconut and thyme soup Page 116	Swede, coconut and thyme soup Page 116
Dinner	Smoked turkey rasher and mushroom carbonara Page 168	Beef casserole Page 142	Beef casserole Page 142
Snacks	Rice cakes	Protein ball Page 217	Carrot sticks and hummus Page 214

Thursday	Friday	Saturday	Sunday
Berry and peanut butter oats Page 96	**2 boiled eggs**	**Poached eggs with a smoky bacon and paprika sweet potato hash** Page 104	**Full Irish** Page 102
Turkey yuk sung Page 118	**Turkey yuk sung** Page 118	**Couscous** Page 206	**Swede, coconut and thyme soup** Page 116
Chicken and tarragon broth Page 158	**Roast hake with a ham and petits pois salsa** Page 176	**Shrimp and pea fried rice** Page 178	**Shrimp and pea fried rice** Page 178
Carrot sticks and hummus Page 214	**Rice cakes**	**Roasted chickpea bites** Page 218	**Kinder Bueno**

Cook in batches

Go to your local shop, pound shop or Ikea and pick up the vital tools called Tupperware. They will have to become your best friend as they will help you lose weight. Fail to prepare – prepare to fail. Repeat that over and over in your head. Make a plan of what you want to eat for the next three days for breakfast, lunch and dinner and make that. It is much easier to stay on track when you are hungry and you will just have to reheat what's in the lunch box. For example, on a Sunday prepare the following staples for the week ahead:

- Marinara sauce
- Swede, coconut and thyme soup
- Hummus
- Couscous
- Beef casserole

Stop with the silly calories

Reduce your lattes and sweetened drinks down to herbal teas and some black coffee – you can still allow for one latte per day but swap the milk to skinny. Don't go for white bread when you can have brown bread. Don't pick at foods that your kids are eating. Start reading labels so you can try and reduce the amount of ingredients that go into something, for example if you are buying passata, try to get one with 100 per cent tomatoes.

Eat every three hours

When you're serious about losing weight, it's important to not let yourself get hungry to the point of being hangry. If this happens, you will pick the wrong food and probably overeat. So make sure you eat regularly and if you know you'll be out and about for a good while prepare to have the right snacks with you.

Do not under any circumstances buy a multipack of crisps of chocolate and tell yourself that you will only have one. If you can identify that you will overeat them then leave them in the shop.

Cut out alcohol

This isn't forever but cut out alcohol for a few weeks and get your body into the right frame of mind. There is no point if you are being good for five days and then at the weekend downing pints or a bottle of wine. You have to give it your all. Protect your weight loss at all times – if you have a friend and the only thing that you do together is eat cake or drink loads then you will have to change your friendship habits or avoid that person for a while.

Buy a nice water bottle and stay hydrated

Personally, I think that this is a vital part of your journey. Water helps you flush out all the toxins that are around your body. It makes sense – if you shower the outside of your body, you must shower the inside of your body. Don't start with an unrealistic goal of 3 litres per day; start with 1.5 litres, get that right and gradually when that is your new norm add on another 100ml and build it up that way. Water helps my skin, my energy and I just feel like I am smashing my day when I am consistent with my water. Buy a nice water bottle – my favourite one is a Nike one as I love the easiness of the drinking. If these things work for you like they do for me then spend the money on a water bottle. The most annoying thing about having a bottle that you love is losing it – I have spent the last 18 months around Cork running back into shops for my forgotten water bottle!

4
Research how you will exercise

A lot of people will ask me what is the most important thing for weight loss, diet or exercise? The truth is you cannot have one without the other. Exercise is vital for losing weight. It will help your mental health tremendously and your body will start using up your fat as fuel; in turn, you will lose your weight.

Evaluate your budget

See what you can afford. If you can afford a gym and a personal trainer, I would highly recommend that. It will take away that scary image that the gym has and it will start to instil confidence within you around weights and cardio machines. If you cannot afford a gym then invest in a good pair of runners and head out for brisk walks, not strolls. You should raise your heart rate and make sure that you aren't able to take a phone call as you would sound weird panting down the phone.

Find your favourite podcast

I'll be honest, motivational pop music to go with workouts just makes me panic! Instead, I listen to podcasts. Here are my current top ten:

1   The Trisha and Dan Show (my own podcast with Dan!)
2   The Brian Keane Podcast
3   The Paul Dermody Podcast
4   West Cork (not weight loss related but brilliant and will keep you walking)
5   The Joe Rogan Experience
6   The GaryVee Audio Experience
7   Bite Back with Rozanna Purcell
8   The 2 Johnnies Podcast
9   The Blindboy Podcast
10   Any podcast with Gerry Hussey!

Top tips when starting with a new trainer

1. **Trust them.** This is their job, they know what they are doing. They are not judging you and they don't care that you don't know what a dumbbell is – they just want to help. Know that you will hate them at some stage but they are human so give them a chance and you will get used to their style of training.

2. **Communicate with your trainer.** If you are tired, tell them. If the weight is too heavy, tell them. If you are paranoid about a certain part of your body, tell them. Build a relationship.

3. **If your trainer isn't working for you, communicate with yourself.** Do not give up, just change the trainer. A good personal trainer will understand if it's not a good fit and they will only want what is best for you. I hate lunges and I am not forced into doing them but I will do them when I want to. Play fair with your trainer.

4. **Keep in mind that it is just as awkward for them in the first few weeks too.** Give the relationship a chance. Build on it.

5. **If you need a cry go for it.** It will happen but do not give up.

Clothes

Don't worry if you don't have the latest gym gear or a sports bra. I am still searching for a sports bra. Just get in and start sweating. Leave your issues at the door and when it's your time just go smash the workout. Know that the exercise will never ever get easier – but you will get stronger.

Take it slow

At the start of my journey, for the first six months, I exercised three times a week for 30 minutes in the gym. In that six months I did maybe 10 extra walks, no more. Once I watched my diet and incorporated a small bit of exercise it was enough for me to go into a calorie deficit and start losing stones. Do not go too hard on yourself with exercise as it is scary when you are unfit. Take it slow and make sure you are enjoying your exercise.

5
Be kind to yourself

Communicate

The best thing about my weight loss journey was the relationships that I formed with my family. Your family will have been suffering too, worrying about you, so communicate with them and keep them updated on your losses and your gains.

Social media – the ultimate highlight reel

Okay, social media can be awesome and fun and a world crammed with billions of people but it can often feel like the loneliest place in the world. My advice to you is to reduce the amount of people you follow. (Don't unfollow me, ha ha!) Always remember that it is just a highlight reel of people's lives. It is very easy to feel sad, jealous or angry at someone's perfect life online. No matter how real an account, it is still filtered. Follow people that make you smile, that make you want to change, that make you feel good after watching them. Don't send abuse, don't send your opinion if it isn't asked for and don't criticise someone online. Don't join hate groups, just smile and live your life. Social media can help you be inspired but if you find it is draining you, turn off your phone and go for a walk.

Turn off your phone

This may seem very ironic coming from me when I spend a lot of time on Instagram but when it comes to winding down turn off your phone two hours before bed so your mind has a chance to switch off and you can get a good night's sleep.

Sleep

The last point brings me nicely onto this point. Go to bed. Turn off Netflix and get that extra hour's rest. Sleep is so vital for this. If I do not get a good night's sleep, the next day I am more prone to picking, I am generally too tired to work out and my recovery isn't as quick as it should be. Kitchen pickers wear bigger knickers – strong girls wear thongs!

Take it slowly

This is my final point and one that I feel so strongly about. Don't look ahead, just take it day by day. Make sure you are organised and focus on the day you have at hand. If you mess up then forgive yourself, move on and reset. If you ruin your breakfast that does not and will not give you the right to ruin your lunch.

Home truths

As I've already said, communication with loved ones is key when starting your weight-loss journey. I thought that there would be no better people to talk about this topic than the people who have been with me since day one – my sisters. My bond with them, their families (and especially all my godchildren!) is so strong.

I asked Kellie, Carol, Michelle, Annie and Maura what they remembered about those years and their responses blew me away.

- 'I really worried about her mental health and she would always be the loudest and most fun but I could always see that was a huge front and she was in a lot of pain.'
- 'I worried about her secret eating. She was in denial about the calories. I knew that she knew I knew and it used to break my heart when I would come home late and she was eating on her own.'
- 'I was always on edge when I was with her because of fear of people insulting her and being mean.'
- 'She was my first best friend. I knew that Trisha was not living her life to the fullest and I knew that she was so unhappy. I tried and tried every moment I could to get the lightbulb moment happen, from her late teens to her twenties.'
- 'I was enjoying my youth and at the same time my baby sister was living a nightmare of staying in and not being sociable.'
- 'Once she put her mind to anything she would succeed. I knew she was brave and full of courage.'
- 'Weight nearly took you from us but I am so glad you were the bravest girl we know.'
- 'I would wake in the night with sheer panic and fear. My chest would be so tight.'

Here is their advice for helping someone you love realise that they can beat the bulge!

- 'Be kind. Be patient. Be there.'
- 'Be a comforting companion, especially when others can be ignorant or cruel.'
- 'Stand up for them. Always have their back.'
- 'Know that no matter how many times they need to start over, the most important thing is that they DO start over.'
- 'Get on every bandwagon, because one of them will be the Rolls Royce.'
- 'If you're going to intervene, have a game plan.'
- 'It's easier said than done. It will be hard knowing that you will hurt them when you are trying to help them.'
- 'Tread the waters carefully and try and say it to them subtly or encouragingly.'
- 'Do not say it when they are eating or in any way down.'
- 'Never give up hope. Trisha had lost hope so we had to keep believing that she would be okay.'
- 'Say it when they are happy and encouraged as opposed to down.'
- 'We often spoke at length about how someday she would become the girl with the before and after photos and how she would write a book. I am glad that her dreams have come true.'

My RECIPE FOR SUCCESS

Ownership

Accept that you have gained the weight, you have eaten the food and you haven't worked out. Yes, sometimes people have hurt you, but you must move on.

Self-love

This is vital. Stop thinking of what you cannot do, think of what you can do. If you can't squat, believe that you can do it. Be proud that you have made the decision to be a transformer. Be proud that you are overweight and you have all the power.

Discipline

Make the decision to start and stick to it. Always remember that staying in bed or skipping the gym session is never worth it. It will be awful; you will have anxiety about it but at the end you will not regret giving yourself the gift of exercise.

Be selfish

If someone or something is not supporting your end goal, then you have to be selfish. You don't have to be cruel but you must make sure you are okay. If you do not treat yourself as number one this will not work. If you have the gym and someone asks you for a favour at that time, put yourself first and say 'no'. It is a simple two-letter word that will be beneficial to you and those who love you.

Know that you are not alone

You may think that you are the only one that overeats, you may think that you are the only one who can't control what goes into your mouth, you are the only one who feels sad. You are not alone.

Set goals

You don't have to do a target of 100 lbs. Set some small realistic targets. If it's a goal of drinking 2 litres of water per day then do that and stick to it. Slowly each week add onto your goals.

Know that sometimes you will fail

Failure is part of life and it will happen. You will mess up. You will overeat. You will gain weight in the middle; you will skip a gym session. You will get drunk and have some chips but accept that and move on. One bad meal will not ruin your journey, but your mind will.

Stop looking at things negatively

This will be hard at the start. You have spent months and years of looking at your weight as a negative. Look at it now as the challenge of your life. It's now time to play a game where there is only one player and that is you. It is you versus you, so be kind to you. You want to be the world champion at your game so build yourself up.

Stay organised

Fail to prepare, prepare to fail. Keep repeating this in your head. You must have the organisation of a weekly shop; you have to organise the times you are going to exercise. You have a goal now and a responsibility to give yourself your energy and your smile back.

Ditch the self-pity

You cannot feel pity and sadness anymore, it's shoulda, woulda, coulda time. The past is in the past. Focus on this exact moment. If you feel sad or depressed about your weight remind yourself that you are living in the past, and if you are worried and riddled in the anxiety about losing weight remind yourself that you are borrowing anxiety from the future. Live in the now and smile. You are alive, you are above the ground.

Silence your inner bully

This is your inside bully; this is the voice that is telling you that you are fat and ugly and you have gone too far. If you tell a teacher on the bully it will instantly become smaller and less scary. Sit down and make a deal with yourself that you cannot think negatively anymore. The damage is done and accept that was out of your control. What you have to accept is that fixing it is now your responsibility.

Only allow supporters in your front door

This includes yourself. If someone doesn't believe that you will do this then just avoid this negativity.

Leave past hurt behind

Use the stones that were fired at you to build your mansion. Don't fire them back to hurt the ones who threw them, just accept that this happened and use them as an advantage. Don't be angry at the people who hurt you and let hatred go. Hating someone or being angry at someone is like you drinking poison and expecting the other person to die. It's not worth it.

Have your treats

As I've said before, the danger's in the dose! So have your bag of chips, but order a small bag and savour them, don't gobble them in a second. Enjoy the treat then move on. You cannot approach this new lifestyle with the attitude that you will never go out again, never eat chips, never drink wine. You will and that's life, it's all about what's happening the rest of your week.

Educate yourself on food

Start reading labels. The purest food is the best. If there are too many ingredients in a simple item it's a red flag.

Stop the lying

You are lying to yourself and lying to others. When you lie about not going for your exercise or the amount of food you have eaten the only person that you are fooling is yourself.

Take it day by day

Do not look ahead. Do not think that you have loads to lose. Retrain your mind that you have a new day to gain. Start in the morning and take each moment step by step and at the end of the day re-evaluate.

Know that it will be hard

This will not be easy but I can promise you if you give it your all you will be so grateful and it will be the greatest present you will ever have.

And the last one that I have is *get over it!*

It's hard, it's tiring, you're upset but you can fix it! Beat the bulge!

A NOTE ON CALORIE COUNTING

I made a decision from the very start that I didn't want to over-complicate things. I had tried calorie-counting diets in the past and they had obviously not been successful. I was so low the day I started this I said that I would just go with the healthy eating approach as opposed to overthinking the whole thing. I loved the freedom of making my own decisions. I didn't go freestyle though – I also made sure that I was making conscious decisions and making myself aware of the calories in the food and checking labels. Here are a few things I keep in mind:

1 **Check how many calories are in the whole pack** – do not check the calories per serving and look at the smaller number. This can confuse you, and if you overeat you don't know what you have eaten.

2 **Check the ingredients** – the fewer ingredients the better.

3 **If you cannot pronounce it or spell it then in general do not eat it!** For example, when buying peanut butter I will always go for 100 per cent nuts as opposed to ones with lots of ingredients that aren't even close to nuts in it.

4 **To get a teaspoon-size of the amount of sugar in something, look at the sugar content and divide by four** – so if it is 8g of sugar I would work it out that it would have two teaspoons of sugar in it.

5 **Ask yourself would you feed this to a newborn or a toddler?** Sometimes you wouldn't dream of feeding a child what you're eating but we find it acceptable to eat it ourselves.

6 **Life is for living and sometimes a Malteser bunny is the best thing you can have.** The key is stopping it at one piece. You will have got the satisfaction from the first and you're just being a bit mad eating the seventh one.

7 **Eat like your life depends on it,** because it does!

8 **Don't be fooled into thinking that protein bars are healthy** – they are chocolate bars with some extra protein added. You can use this as your treat but remember that they are still chocolate bars. Sometimes I would prefer to have an extra chicken breast or a spud as this usually will fill me up and keep me satisfied for longer!

9 **Be careful on your coffees** – if you are drinking four lattes per day and wondering why you aren't losing weight it means that you are not being accountable. Reduce to one per day and swap the full-fat milk for skinny milk.

10 **Focus on being healthy and get yourself started, don't overthink it.** It is not a race; this needs to be sustainable for the rest of your life so make sure you enjoy it.

11 **Once every two weeks I go onto the MyFitnessPal calorie-tracking app** and log everything that I am eating to make sure that I am on track and I am not going mad on portions. This is vital. You could be eating all the healthy food in the world but you could be overeating on calories. It's all about changing your mindset and approaching food with respect and love. This app will give you valuable feedback on where you are going wrong.

BREAKFAST

I am always at my hungriest in the morning so a good breakfast is vital for me.
Just after breakfast I start my 40-minute commute to the gym and work so if
I am hungry going up in the car, I am usually low in energy! Before I used to
make a mistake of not eating for four or five hours after I got up and I would
eat a huge meal at lunch so I was stodgy. Breakfast for me usually is one of
two things: oats or eggs. Try and avoid ready-made meals like instant porridge
and shop-bought granolas as they are usually laced in sugar, which will make
you crave more bad food. I like to make sure my breakfasts only take a few
minutes to make so I can avoid the age-old excuse that I have no time! A cup
of hot water and a half a lemon to cleanse yourself and a healthy breakfast will
make the day much easier. If you want to make your breakfast more exciting at
the weekend then I would look at the Full Irish (see page 102).

**PREP
TIME**

**COOKING
TIME**

SERVES

VEGETARIAN

**GLUTEN
FREE**

BERRY AND PEANUT BUTTER OATS

Being honest, I don't really like oats in general but they make me feel so good
I had to make them work for me. So I added some extra ingredients –
who doesn't like berries? I'm happy to say it is absolutely delicious now!
I am just set up for the day with this nourishing bowl.

35g oats

150ml full fat milk

50g frozen raspberries

60g fresh strawberries,
   hulled and halved

40g fresh raspberries

20g fresh blueberries

15g 100% peanut butter

Put your oats and milk in a pot and bring to the boil.
Turn down the heat and cook for 2 minutes, stirring
continuously until thickened.

Add in your frozen raspberries and cook until soft and
heated through.

Tip into a bowl and scatter over your fresh strawberries,
blueberries and raspberries, then spoon the peanut
butter on top.

5 MINS   **8 MINS**   1

My go-to breakfast

RASPBERRY AND COCONUT SMOOTHIE BOWL

—————|—————

This is so yummy and easy to whizz up and it makes breakfast more exciting. The frozen raspberries will naturally bring a nice chill to your smoothie.

—————|—————

100g natural yoghurt
50g frozen raspberries
25g desiccated coconut
   (plus more to garnish)
2 tsp honey
1 tsp vanilla extract
10g almond butter
20ml almond milk

To garnish:
desiccated coconut, lightly
   toasted on a dry pan
fresh raspberries
fresh strawberries, sliced
blueberries
5 fresh mint leaves

Blitz all the ingredients in a blender. Tip into a bowl and garnish with some coconut, raspberries, strawberries, blueberries and fresh mint leaves

5 MINS   1

TRISHA'S TIP

If you're using fresh raspberries, add some ice into your blender to make it nice and cold.

GRANOLA

———

Although they look healthy, shop-bought granolas can be laden with sugar which won't help you in the long run if you are trying to lose weight. This is so gorgeous! Store in an airtight container and enjoy the delicious smell of the kitchen after it comes from the oven! Please be aware that nuts are high in fat but they are healthy fats. Just make sure you don't go crazy on the serving!

———

70g oats
100g sunflower seeds
80g walnuts
100g pumpkin seeds
165g flaked almonds
200g desiccated coconut
150g dried cranberries

Preheat your oven to 180°C.

Combine all your ingredients, except for the cranberries, in a big bowl and mix well.

Spread the mixture out on a large baking tray and make sure it isn't heaped in any places, as that will stop the bottom bits from toasting properly.

Put in the oven for 20 minutes, then remove and stir everything around. Return to the oven for another 5 minutes, until everything looks nicely golden and crunchy.

Once out of the oven, stir your cranberries through. Let cool, then store in an airtight container.

5 MINS   **25 MINS**   **20 PORTIONS**

BANANA PANCAKES

Most people love a good pancake! The good news is this recipe isn't too crazy on calories so you can enjoy them with no guilt. Have these on a lazy Sunday morning – if you double the batch you can freeze them!

Blitz the bananas, vanilla extract, cinnamon and eggs in a blender or in a bowl with a stick blender until a smooth batter is formed.

Heat some coconut oil in a medium-sized non-stick pan. Dollop ¼ of the mixture into the pan. Do not agitate the pan, just cook it until one side of the pancake becomes golden brown. Flip over with a spatula and finish cooking. Keep warm while you cook the remainder of the pancakes in the same way.

Serve these on their own, or with any of the garnish suggestions.

2 bananas
1 tsp vanilla extract
½ tsp cinnamon
4 free range eggs
1 tsp coconut oil, for frying

To garnish:
fresh berries
melted dark chocolate
    and orange slices
toasted walnuts and
    agave syrup
caramelised bananas

5 MINS   10 MINS   2

TRISHA'S FULL IRISH

———

If you're trying to eat healthily, it doesn't mean you have to miss out on the classic Full Irish we all know and love. In my version, you are simply being cute and swapping ingredients out for healthier versions.

———

light spray
2 turkey sausages
2 turkey rashers
5 mushrooms, sliced
1 tomato, halved
2 free range eggs
1 portion of homemade
  baked beans
  (see page 134)

Spray a non-stick frying pan with some oil and fry off your sausages, rashers and mushrooms. Alternatively, pop them on a George Foreman grill. Keep warm while you prepare the rest of the breakfast.

Heat up your baked beans.

Grill the tomato and boil the eggs for 5–6 minutes, depending on how runny you like your yolk.

Serve everything together and devour with a cup of hot tea.

2 MINS　　**15 MINS**　　**1**

This is simply delicious for your weekend treat!

POACHED EGGS
WITH A SMOKY BACON AND PAPRIKA SWEET POTATO HASH

This is a delicious brunch–style dish, one that is a colourful and packed full of vitamins and protein. Great for those lazy Sunday mornings when you need the break from routine weekday breakfasts without ruining your weight loss.

2 medium-sized sweet
   potatoes, cubed but not
   peeled
1 tbsp olive oil
2 tsp smoked paprika
salt and black pepper
2 smoked rashers (visible
   fat removed), chopped
2 garlic cloves, finely
   chopped
½ a red onion, chopped
   into large chunks
6 cherry tomatoes
4 free range eggs
1 tsp vinegar
a handful of fresh spinach,
   washed and shredded

Preheat your oven to 180°C.

Put your sweet potato in a bowl and toss together with the oil, seasoning, chopped rashers, garlic and red onion. Spread the mixture out on a baking tray and roast for 25 minutes, stirring halfway through.

Five minutes before it's finished cooking, pop your tomatoes, sprinkled with some salt, onto the tray to lightly roast.

To make the eggs, pop a pot of water over a high heat and bring it to the boil. Reduce this to a simmer and add in a pinch of salt and the vinegar. Crack an egg into a cup. Swirl the water lightly and slip in your egg. Repeat for the rest of the eggs. Take out with a spoon when your eggs are cooked the way you like them – I like mine after 3 minutes.

Take your sweet potato and tomatoes from the oven and mix the shredded spinach through. Divide between two plates, and pop the poached eggs and some of the roasted tomatoes on top.

10 MINS   **30 MINS**   **2**

This dish is one to impress your friends with when they are over for brunch. The colours are so vibrant and you will feel so good eating it!

POACHED EGGS
WITH PEA GUACAMOLE, CHILLI AND FETA CHEESE

———

This is a perfect dish for a lazy weekend brunch.
The sweetness of the peas matched with the spice of the chilli and the
saltiness of the feta makes it a winning combination. Just leave out the rashers for
a vegetarian feast.

———

100g frozen peas
juice of 1 lemon
2 tsp olive oil
1 red onion, diced
2 red chillies, diced
a handful of fresh basil,
   chopped
2 free range eggs
2 turkey rashers
2 slices of sourdough bread
20g feta cheese

Pop on 2 pots of salted water to boil. Put the peas in one pot. Once the water starts boiling take out your peas with a slotted spoon and put them in a bowl of cold water for a minute. This (called 'blanching') will ensure your peas stay lovely and green. Then pop them in a bowl with the lemon juice, olive oil, diced red onion, diced red chillies and fresh basil. Mix well to combine, crushing the peas a bit as you go to create a rough pesto consistency.

Poach your eggs (see page 104 for instructions).

Grill your turkey rashers.

To assemble your brunch, toast the sourdough bread and divide between two plates. Spread your pea guacamole on each slice and add your rashers and poached eggs and crumble your feta cheese on top.

5 MINS   **20 MINS**   **2**

SMOKED SALMON MUFFINS

———————

These muffins are so simple to make but so effective in satisfying your palate. Breakfast, lunch or dinner these can be used for! Serve with some salad and hummus if you would like a more substantial meal.

———————

130g self-raising flour
100ml low-fat milk
30g butter, melted
1 egg, beaten
200g smoked salmon, chopped
110g Parmesan cheese, grated
1 tsp fresh or dried parsley
1 tsp fresh or dried thyme
black pepper
1 egg beaten with some milk (egg wash)

Preheat your oven to 180°C. Grease a 24-cup muffin tin or line with paper cases.

Sieve your flour and baking powder into a large bowl. Add milk, butter and the egg and stir until smooth.

Add the smoked salmon, Parmesan, parsley, thyme and pepper. Fold to combine well.

Use a soup spoon to pop your mixture evenly into each well of your muffin tin (or paper case if using). Brush some egg wash over the top of each muffin to add a nice shine, then pop in the preheated oven for 15–20 minutes. After this time, use a knife to pierce the middle of a muffin and if it comes back clean they are done.

Leave on a cooling rack until cool. You can keep these in the fridge for 2 days or you can freeze them and defrost as you go.

10 MINS **20 MINS** **24 MUFFINS**

SWEETCORN ROSTI

I love this dish as it's a healthy, funky breakfast that can also double up as a good lunch. You can make this more substantial by topping with some poached eggs or you can serve with a simple rocket and feta salad with some house dressing (see page 192) for lunch. It is cheap and reheats well. This mix can be made in advance or used straight away.

In a bowl or jug, mix in half of your sweetcorn, the milk, eggs and chilli and blitz with a stick blender until smooth.

Fold in your flour, cayenne pepper, spring onion, spinach and salt and pepper and mix well. Stir in the remaining sweetcorn to give your rosti more of a texture.

Heat some oil in a pan and fry the rosti gently on a medium heat until the underside is golden. Flip over carefully and cook until the other side is also crispy and golden brown.

Serve cut into wedges.

150g tinned sweetcorn, drained
1 tbsp milk
2 free range eggs
½ a red chilli, diced
40g plain flour
¼ tsp cayenne pepper
1 spring onion, finely diced
100g spinach
salt and black pepper
oil for frying

10 MINS   **5 MINS**   **4**

LUNCH

The main thing that I do differently now when the lunch cravings arrive is to always have a lunch ready with me. There are two main benefits of this: you have full control of your diet and it is so much cheaper than spending €8 to €15 on your lunch daily. Invest in Tupperware! I usually use my dinner leftovers from the night before and heat them up for my lunch, or I'll batch cook and have the same thing for a few days – so easy to just grab from the fridge and reheat. If I am stuck and I end up having to go to a deli, I will pick a brown wrap, plain chicken, peppers and some onions and I get them to toast it really well so it goes from a boring wrap to a crunchy, toasted one! If I find myself in a supermarket, I will usually pick up some sort of Greek yoghurt, a piece of fruit and a pack of precooked chicken from the shelf. Avoid breaded chicken and sugary yoghurts or premade salad boxes that you have no control over. And save the chicken roll for the hangover!

PREP TIME

COOKING TIME

SERVES

VEGETARIAN

GF
GLUTEN FREE

CHICKEN AND SWEETCORN SOUP

Of all the Chinese soups I get in takeaways, this one is my favourite.
You wouldn't think it was easy to recreate the delicious taste at home,
but try my version and you'll find that it is! It can also be
whipped up in less than 15 minutes!

3 reduced-salt chicken
   stock cubes
1 litre boiling water
2 skinless chicken breasts,
   diced
260g tinned sweetcorn,
   drained
1 tbsp sesame oil*
2 tbsp reduced-salt soy
   sauce
2 free range eggs, whisked
5 spring onions, thinly
   sliced (reserve one for
   garnish)

In a big pot, dissolve your three chicken stock cubes in the boiling water. Reduce to a simmer.

Add in your diced chicken pieces and simmer for 6 minutes, until they have turned from pink to white.

Add in the sweetcorn and simmer for another 5 minutes, then add in the sesame oil and soy sauce, stirring continuously.

Stir the whisked eggs into the mix – this will make your soup cloudy. Simmer for another 2 minutes.

Add in your chopped spring onions and serve in a bowls, garnished with more spring onions.

*If you don't want too much oil, you could use half the amount of sesame oil and substitute it with sesame seeds or tahini.

5 MINS **15 MINS** **4**

CHICKEN NOODLE SOUP

I love this warming broth that can be eaten as dinner, or as a lunch
in a smaller portion. It's high in protein and will warm you to your toes
when it's cold and wet outside.

2 reduced-salt chicken stock
   cubes
500ml boiling water
2 skinless chicken breasts,
   sliced
1 tsp garlic purée
1 onion, sliced
2 tsp reduced-salt soy sauce
100g frozen peas
1 red chilli, diced (optional, if
   you like it spicy)
100g noodles
a bunch of fresh parsley,
   chopped
lime wedges
3 spring onions, finely
   chopped

In a medium-sized pot dissolve your stock cubes in the boiling
water. Add in your sliced chicken, turn the heat down to a
simmer, and gently poach the chicken until it is cooked through.

Add in your garlic purée, onion and soy sauce and simmer
gently for 10 minutes.

Next add your frozen peas, chilli (if using) and noodles and
simmer for another 3 minutes.

Finish by scattering over your chopped parsley, lime wedges
and spring onions. Divide between two bowls.

5 MINS   **30 MINS**   **2**

TRISHA'S TIP

Be careful that you get noodles that are not pre-fried, as this this will add unnecessary calories.

SWEDE, COCONUT AND THYME SOUP

This is a vegan-friendly soup. I have replaced the cream with coconut milk to reduce calories, but don't worry if you're not a fan of coconut – the rich flavour of the soup will overwhelm any strong coconut flavour.

1 tbsp olive oil
3 onions, chopped
8 garlic cloves, chopped
6 sticks of celery, chopped
2 small swedes/turnips, trimmed and chopped
500ml water
3 reduced-salt vegetable stock cubes
1 400g tin of light coconut milk
1 bunch of fresh thyme, leaves picked
1 tsp mustard powder
salt and black pepper

In a large soup pot, sweat off your onions, garlic and celery in the oil over a medium heat until they become soft and see-through.

Add in your swede or turnip. Pour in your water gradually, to about an inch below your vegetables. Take your time with this step – you can always add more liquid in, but you can't take it out.

Crumble in your stock cubes and simmer for 20 minutes.

After 20 minutes add in your tin of coconut milk, the thyme and the mustard powder. Boil for 5 minutes, then remove from the heat and blitz your soup with a stick blender. Season to taste accordingly.

This soup will last for up to 3 days in the fridge, or freeze immediately once it is cool; it will defrost well.

10 MINS   **40 MINS**   **8**

TURKEY YUK SUNG

This is my favourite dish to get in the Chinese. It is so tasty, I had to find out how to make it at home! The key here is to have crunchy, fresh iceberg lettuce. The turkey mix is easily reheated so you can make it in batches.

½ tsp coconut oil

1 onion, diced

5 garlic cloves, minced

400g turkey mince

6 button mushrooms, sliced

½ a red pepper, deseeded and chopped

1 inch of fresh ginger, peeled and
   chopped

4 tsp reduced-salt soy sauce

1 tsp sesame oil

4 spring onions, sliced

½ an iceberg lettuce, leaves separated
   and washed

For the yoghurt dressing:

60g natural yoghurt

2 tsp garlic purée

2 tsp sriracha sauce

juice of ½ a lemon

To garnish:

1 red chilli, finely chopped

sesame seeds

In a large pan, sauté the onion and garlic in the coconut oil over a medium heat until softened. Add in your turkey mince, mushrooms and pepper. Use a spatula to mix the mince around until browned. Add in the ginger and cook for 8 minutes.

Add in the soy sauce, sesame oil and spring onions.

To make the yoghurt dressing, mix all the ingredients together in a bowl.

Now you're ready to assemble your yuk sung. Scoop a dollop of your hot mix into a lettuce leaf, using it like a cup. Top with some yoghurt dressing and garnish with chilli and sesame seeds.

5 MINS   **15 MINS**   **2**

CHICKEN CAESAR SALAD

The nicest salad that exists, in my opinion. Usually it is laden in calories but using my Caesar dressing recipe will make it a guilt-free lunch! To make this recipe, you'll need a batch of my dressing (page 188).

1 bagel (for croutons)

1 tsp olive oil

2 garlic cloves, sliced

2 heads of baby gem lettuce, torn and washed

1 red onion, chopped

50ml Caesar dressing (see page 188)

100g cajun-style chicken, sliced (see page 164)

Preheat the oven to 150°C.

Start by making your croutons. Chop the bagel into small cubes and toss in a small bowl with the olive oil and garlic. Pop on a baking tray and into the preheated oven for 15 minutes, until golden and crispy.

Put your torn baby gem lettuce into a salad bowl and add in your red onion. Mix in your croutons and your Caesar dressing and fold everything together. Divide between two bowls and add the sliced chicken on top.

5 MINS **15 MINS** **2**

TRISHA'S TIP

If you had some leftover roast chicken from Sunday dinner, you could also use it in this recipe.

STICKY CHICKEN SALAD
WITH RED ONION AND CHERRY TOMATOES

I love salads but sometimes they can be so boring and bland.
The acidity from the balsamic vinegar gives this one a special kick and
makes the chicken lovely and sticky.

6 cherry tomatoes

1 tsp olive oil

150g skinless chicken
   breast, sliced

1 tbsp balsamic vinegar

100g fresh spinach, washed
   and shredded

100g rocket, washed

1 red onion, sliced

To garnish:

1 spring onion, sliced

Preheat your oven to 200°C.

Pop your cherry tomatoes on a baking tray lined with baking parchment. Season with sea salt. Pop your tray into the preheated oven and roast the tomatoes for 5 minutes.

Meanwhile, in a wok fry off your chicken in the oil until cooked. Add in your balsamic vinegar and reduce for 1 minute until the chicken is coated and sticky.

In a serving bowl mix your spinach, rocket and red onion. Add your hot chicken mixture on top. Garnish with some spring onion and add the roasted cherry tomatoes on the side.

5 MINS   **15 MINS**   **2**

TUNA SALAD PITTA BREAD

Tuna and sweetcorn is the tired old twosome that people seem to always put together in a sandwich or wrap. Well not me! Here is something different. It is so easy to prepare and can be made in minutes!

1 160g tin of tuna in brine, drained
1 red onion, chopped
8 gherkins, chopped
200g mixed leaves
2 brown pitta pockets
20g light cream cheese

To make your filling, mix your tuna, onion, gherkins and leaves in a small bowl.

Toast your pitta breads, cut open lengthways and spread your light cream cheese on the inside, then stuff with your tuna mix.

5 MINS   **5 MINS**   **2**

SMOKED SALMON PÂTÉ

|—————————|

This super-easy pâté is a go-to recipe of mine. These are great for lunch with the girls or for a starter!

|—————————|

1 tsp coconut oil
2 fillets of skinless salmon
50g light cream cheese
1 tsp fresh chives, chopped
zest of 1 lemon, finely
   chopped
salt and black pepper to
   taste
4 slices of brown bread

To garnish:
a handful of fresh cress,
   chopped
a handful of fresh mint
   leaves, chopped

Preheat your oven to 180°C.

If you have a George Foreman grill, pop the salmon on for 7 minutes, otherwise lightly fry in coconut oil for 1 minute. Then put the salmon fillets into the oven for 10 minutes. Leave to cool.

Flake the cooled salmon into a bowl and mix with cream cheese, chives and lemon zest. Season with salt and black pepper.

Spread onto some brown bread and garnish with some cress and mint leaves.

5 MINS   **12 MINS**   **2**

GRILLED CHICKEN BURGERS
WITH A MUSHROOM AND GREEN PEPPER RAGOUT

I love this dish for a quick low-carbohydrate lunch after the gym. I use loads of mushrooms as they are low in calories and make it feel like a bigger meal. I buy naked (not breaded) chicken burgers in the supermarket with a high percentage of chicken. Using beef tomatoes, which are full of juice, helps create a natural sauce.

2 readymade chicken
   burgers (see above)
spray oil
4 garlic cloves, crushed (or
   4 tsp frozen garlic)
12 button mushrooms
1 green pepper, deseeded
   and chopped
2 beef tomatoes, roughly
   chopped
1 tsp dried thyme
salt and black pepper

Preheat your oven to 180°C.

Fry burgers on both sides on a hot pan to seal and finish on a baking tray in the preheated oven for 20 minutes.

Meanwhile, heat your wok, spray with a little oil and lightly fry off your garlic. Add in your mushrooms and a drop of water to create steam, which will help you control your cooking.

After 2 minutes, add in your green pepper, tomatoes and thyme. Season with salt and pepper and cook until all the veg have become soft and combined.

Serve with your cooked chicken burgers.

3 MINS   **30 MINS**   **2**

CHICKEN QUESADILLA

I love this Mexican dish of cheese and other fillings cooked in a wrap until piping hot and melty. This recipe is quick to prepare if you've already made the Cajun chicken from page 164. For a more substantial lunch, serve with some oven-roasted chips or rocket salad.

Preheat your oven to 180°C.

Lay out your wraps on a board. Scatter all your chopped items over half of each wrap, sprinkle your Cheddar cheese on top and fold them over to make a semicircle.

Brush the top of the quesadilla with some olive oil to give a nice crispy finish, pop on a baking tray and cook in the preheated oven for 15 minutes. Remove from the oven and cut each wrap in half to make four triangles altogether. Serve on their own or with the suggested sides above.

2 white wraps
2 cooked Cajun chicken breasts (see page 164), chopped
1 red onion, finely chopped
4 black olives, chopped
1 red pepper, deseeded and chopped
50g Cheddar cheese, grated
olive oil

5 MINS   15 MINS   2

SAVOURY OMELETTE

An omelette is great for a fast, healthy lunch. When I was in school I worked part-time in The Hunters Rest in Mitchelstown, a restaurant where omelettes had their own space on the menu. I quickly learned how versatile and simple they were to make and they are still my go-to quick, filling dish.

light oil spray
2 turkey rashers, chopped
2 mushrooms, chopped
2 spring onions, sliced
3 cherry tomatoes, halved
2 free range egg whites
1 full free range egg
2 tsp milk
15g feta cheese

Get a non-stick frying pan and spray it with some oil. Fry off your rashers, mushrooms, spring onions and tomatoes. Remove to a plate nearby and wipe out the pan with kitchen paper to prepare it for cooking the eggs. Preheat your grill.

Pop your egg whites, full egg and milk in a bowl and gently mix with a fork until they have all combined.

Spray some more oil on your non-stick pan, tip in your egg mix and leave on the hob for 10 seconds to get a colour on your eggs, then pop under your grill to finish off the cooking from the top down.

Once the egg is cooked and fluffy, arrange your warm mixture of rashers and veg on top, crumble on your feta cheese and fold over. Serve with a rocket salad or some roasted sweet potato.

5 MINS   **10 MINS**   **1**

BAKED POTATOES
WITH A CHILLI CHICKEN FILLING

This dish is a favourite of mine because you just cannot beat having a nice baked spud! This recipe has everything going for it – it is quick and simple, the mix can be ready in the fridge and double up as a filling for a wrap, you can make it in advance and kill two lunches with the one stone! Serve with hummus on the side for a more substantial meal (see page 214).

2 baking potatoes, washed
sea salt
olive oil
salt and black pepper

For the filling:
2 tsp olive oil
1 onion, finely diced
3 garlic cloves, chopped
1 skinless breast of chicken,
    chopped
3 button mushrooms, sliced
1 red pepper, deseeded and
    diced
4 tsp sweet chilli sauce

To garnish:
fresh parsley, chopped

Preheat your oven to 200°C.

Use a sharp knife to prick your spuds all over then score with a cross on the top about 2cm deep. Sprinkle with sea salt and drizzle with olive oil, massaging everything in with your hands.

Pop into the microwave for 3 minutes on full power, turn over and continue cooking for a further 5 minutes. Pop onto a tray and crisp them up in your preheated oven for 12 minutes.

To make your filling, sauté the onion and garlic in a pan with the oil until soft, and then add in your chicken, mushrooms and red pepper. When your chicken is cooked, bind the mix together with your sweet chilli sauce.

Remove the potatoes from the oven, cut open and scoop in the hot filling. Garnish with some chopped fresh parsley and serve.

5 MINS　　**30 MINS**　　**2**

HEALTHY BAKED BEANS
ON SOURDOUGH TOAST WITH CRUMBLED FETA

|——————|

This is a yummy breakfast or brunch. The crumble of feta on top will give the dish a beautiful element of saltiness and add some flavour which is vital when you are eating to promote weight loss.

|——————|

100ml marinara sauce
  (see page 189)
1 400g tin of chickpeas,
  drained
2 slices of sourdough bread
a handful of fresh basil,
  chopped
15g feta
sea salt and black pepper
100g rocket, washed

Pop your marinara sauce in a pot, add in your drained chickpeas and bring to a boil. Leave to simmer for 15 minutes, stirring regularly.

Toast your sourdough and put on two plates.

Add some chopped basil at the very last second of cooking the beans as it will lose its colour and become bitter if it is cooked too much.

Spoon your healthy beans onto your sourdough, crumble your feta on top, then sprinkle with some sea salt and black pepper and finally add some rocket on the side.

6 MINS   **15 MINS**   **2**

TRISHA'S TIP

The beans will last for three days once they are kept in the fridge.

FETA, BROCCOLI, HAZELNUT AND TOMATO SALAD

This colourful, nutritious salad is ideal for a quick lunch on the go. It is really tasty and can be eaten on its own, as a side to a more substantial dinner, or you can big it up with some cooked chicken or salmon.

1 head of broccoli, broken
    into florets
50g hazelnuts, blanched
    (no skin) and crushed
2 beef tomatoes, sliced
50g feta cheese
2 tsp cream
1 tbsp extra virgin olive oil
salt and black pepper

Preheat your oven to 200°C.

Prepare a bowl full of ice-cold water. Pop a pot of water on to boil and once it comes to the boil add in ½ tsp of salt, followed by the broccoli. Once the water starts boiling again take out your broccoli with a slotted spoon and pop it in the bowl of cold water to stop it cooking.

Pop your hazelnuts on a small baking tray and put in the hot oven for a few minutes to roast (you'll need to watch them like a hawk as they burn really quickly!).

In a bowl, mix your feta cheese with a fork – add the cream until it has the consistency of a paste.

Once you have the broccoli, nuts and tomatoes ready, pop them onto a plate, top with the feta and drizzle over your olive oil. Season with the salt and pepper. This will store in the fridge for 2 days.

5 MINS   **15 MINS**   **4**

MUSHROOM AND TARRAGON BRUSCHETTA

This is a simple dish that will take ten minutes to make. The bread should be fresh sourdough or a nice baguette from the supermarket. Great for brunch or lunch – a delicious weekend treat! If you would like to add some eggs for protein this will work too.

1 tsp olive oil
1 onion, chopped
3 garlic cloves, chopped
6 button mushrooms, chopped
2 Portobello mushrooms, chopped
50g light cream cheese
25ml light cream
salt and black pepper
1 tsp fresh or dried tarragon
2 slices of sourdough bread

To garnish:
100g rocket leaves

In a pan, sauté your onion, garlic and both types of mushrooms with the olive oil.

Once this mixture is softened, add in your cream cheese, cream and seasoning. Simmer for 1 minute. Add in your tarragon.

Toast your sourdough and put on two plates. Pile the hot mixture on top of each slice. Garnish with some rocket leaves.

4 MINS **10 MINS** **2**

TRISHA'S TIP

Having just one slice of bread
but loads of mushrooms will
fill you up with no guilt!

DINNER

At dinner time in particular, you can be cute with your carbohydrates. If you turn things from white to brown in general it will be better for you as it is higher in fibre. The only swap that I will not do is rice, as I'm not a fan of brown rice! If you have sauces batch-cooked then you can have a dinner made in minutes. I will often have packs of microwavable rice in the cupboard and have my veg pre-chopped so it is matter of just cooking. When you are finished a long day the last thing you want to do is go peeling onions! Going out for dinner is a tricky one for me. My advice is, if you don't do it often then don't overthink it – one dinner out of the seven you have in a week will not ruin your diet. Just don't do the dog on it – when I am out now, I tend to refuse the bread on arrival and I will try and skip my starter. I will go for fish if the restaurant is good enough or I will get a lean steak like a fillet. I am getting so much better at controlling the fact that my eyes are bigger than my belly.

PREP TIME

COOKING TIME

SERVES

VEGETARIAN

GLUTEN FREE

BEEF CASSEROLE
WITH BABY POTATOES

├─────────────┤

A hot, hearty beef casserole is just so comforting and filling on a cold, damp winter's day. The best part of this dish is that it tastes even better if you have it the next day!

├─────────────┤

1 tsp coconut oil

1 white onion, sliced

2 carrots, chopped

400g lean stewing beef pieces

700ml water

20g gravy granules

2 reduced-salt beef stock cubes

2 tbsp tomato purée

5 bay leaves

1 tsp dried thyme

6 baby potatoes, chopped

10 button mushrooms, sliced

To garnish:

fresh parsley, chopped

Preheat your oven to 160°C.

Put a big stew pot on a medium to high heat and add your coconut oil. Tip in your onion, carrots and stewing beef and stir around until all parts of the meat are nicely browned. Add in the water, gravy granules, stock cubes, tomato purée, bay leaves, thyme, potatoes and mushrooms. Bring to the boil.

Cover with a lid and cook in the preheated oven for 2 hours. The longer you stew, the more tender the meat will become. Garnish with some chopped parsley and serve. There's no need for an accompaniment as the spuds are in the sauce!

15 MINS   **2¹/₂ HOURS**   **8**

BEEF, ONION AND PEA CURRY

———

I love a traditional brown curry. One that Mam would have made for us when we came in the door from school, where the onions were soft and your nose would run with the heat! This recipe is so simple and so quick to make!

———

spray oil

3 onions, sliced

2 garlic cloves, sliced

200g stir-fry beef strips

4 heaped tbsp of
   Funky Monkey curry
   powder (available in
   supermarkets)

2 tsp ground ginger

1 cooking apple, peeled,
   cored and finely chopped

1 red pepper, deseeded and
   chopped

2 reduced-salt chicken
   stock cubes

800ml boiling water

2 tbsp ketchup

2 tbsp tomato purée

75g frozen peas

To garnish:

1 red chilli, finely chopped

1 spring onion, finely
   chopped

Spray a big, non-stick pan with some oil and sauté off your onions, garlic and beef at a high heat. Add in your curry powder, ginger, apple and red pepper.

When the beef is browed and the veg are softened, crumble in your stock cubes and pour over your boiling water. Bring to the boil and leave to simmer for 5 minutes.

Add in your ketchup, tomato purée and frozen peas and when the peas are soft the curry is done! Couldn't be easier! Serve on its own or with rice, and garnish with some chopped chilli and spring onions.

5 MINS   **25 MINS**   **4**

LASAGNE!

―――――

I do only three layers in my lasagne as it saves on time and calories!
You can individually wrap this in portions and have them frozen for a handy dinner
when you've no time to cook.

―――――

600g lean beef mince
2 large onions, chopped
4 garlic cloves, chopped
2 celery sticks, finely chopped
2 carrots, finely chopped
3 tbsp tomato purée
1 400g tin of chopped tomatoes
1 reduced-salt beef stock cube
6 button mushrooms, chopped
1 courgette, finely chopped
1 tsp dried thyme
salt and black pepper
spray oil
12 lasagne sheets
½ jar of shop-bought white
   sauce (about 220g)
10g grated Parmesan cheese

Preheat your oven to 180°C.

In a pan fry the mince, onions, garlic and celery, stirring the beef around regularly until it has browned nicely. Add in your carrots, tomato purée, tin of tomatoes, stock cube, mushrooms, courgette, thyme and salt and pepper. Simmer in the pan for 10 minutes.

Spray the bottom of a lasagne pan with some oil and line it with a layer of lasagne sheets. Follow with a layer of the mince mixture and a layer of white sauce. Continue to layer lasagne, mince and white sauce, finishing with a white sauce layer. Sprinkle the Parmesan over the top.

Bake in the preheated oven for 40 minutes. Cut into portions and serve with a nice green salad.

15 MINS　**60 MINS**　**6**

SPAGHETTI BOLOGNESE

Quite simply, one of my favourite dishes in the world. My biggest downfall is going back to the pot for more, so when you are plating this up pop the remainder away asap! Lovely served with a rocket salad and my house dressing (page 192).

Sauté the onion, garlic, blitzed carrot, mince and rosemary in a pan until the mince turns completely brown, stirring regularly.

Mix in your marinara sauce and red wine and simmer gently for 25 minutes, adding salt and pepper to taste.

Meanwhile, cook the pasta following the packet instructions and drain. Serve the Bolognese on a bed of spaghetti and enjoy!

1 onion, diced
3 garlic cloves, minced
3 carrots, blitzed in a
  blender
250g lean beef mince
2 tsp dried rosemary
150ml marinara sauce (see
  page 189)
50ml red wine
salt and black pepper
100g spaghetti

5 MINS   35 MINS   2

- 147 -

MEXICAN-STYLE PANCAKES

|—————|

If you want to have a yummy dinner that will keep your taste buds satisfied and impress guests, this is an ideal dish. It is healthy and still tasty! The beef mix can be made in advance and used in batches.

|—————|

spray oil
1 onion, sliced
2 garlic cloves, chopped
200g lean stir-fry beef strips
4 button mushrooms, sliced
1 red chilli, finely chopped
1 tsp Cajun spices
1 tsp cayenne pepper
1 tsp ground cumin
100ml passata
2 tbsp marinara sauce (see page 189)
salt and black pepper
2 wholemeal wraps
30g Cheddar cheese
100g rocket, washed
house dressing (page 192)

To garnish:
thyme, chopped

Preheat your oven to 180°C.

Spray your wok with a little oil and stir-fry your onion and garlic. Add in your beef strips and sear. Don't agitate the pan; just let the beef colour – you don't want it to boil and stew and become too chewy.

Add in your mushrooms, chilli and spices and cook for 1 minute. Add in your passata and marinara sauce and simmer for 6 minutes. Season to taste with salt and pepper.

Place your wraps on a board and divide the mixture between them. Roll each wrap so that the edges are overlapping and no contents are spilling out. Pop them on a baking tray and sprinkle your cheese on top. Bake in the oven for 12 minutes, garnish with chopped thyme and serve with rocket salad and my house dressing.

10 MINS   **35 MINS**   **2**

TRISHA'S TIP

Use tender, high quality
meat for this recipe

ASIAN-STYLE SALMON COUSCOUS

This is a healthy, delightful dinner. Couscous is a grain that is so adaptable to many flavours and can be made sweet or savoury. You can eat this dish hot or cold, and it reheats well. Added to that, it is high in protein, which is necessary for growth and repair.

200g couscous
1 reduced-salt fish stock cube
300ml boiling water
2 tsp sesame oil
1 tsp garlic purée
400g lean skinless salmon
50g frozen petits pois
1 red pepper, deseeded and diced
1 red onion, diced

To garnish:
fresh mint, chopped
lime wedges

Preheat your oven to 180°C.

Put the couscous in a bowl, crumble in the stock cube and pour over the boiling water. Cover tightly with cling film and leave sit for 5 minutes to allow the grains to absorb the water and swell.

Rub your sesame oil and garlic purée on your salmon and bake on a baking tray in your oven for 20 minutes,

Lightly sauté your peas, red pepper and onion in a pan until the veg are cooked but crunchy. Combine with your couscous (which will have plumped up beautifully), pop a piece of salmon on top and garnish with some fresh mint and lime wedges.

5 MINS **30 MINS** **3**

SPICY MEATBALLS IN A TOMATO STEW

This dish is bursting with fibre and protein. You can make it in big batches and freeze portions to be used when you don't have time to cook but fancy a delicious, hearty dinner. Serve with rice or potatoes or as a pasta sauce.

12 5%-fat meatballs
   (available from your
   supermarket or butcher)
1 red onion, diced
6 garlic cloves
1 red chilli, chopped
3 mushrooms, sliced
1 400g tin of chopped
   tomatoes
1 400g tin of passata
1 400g tin of butter beans,
   drained
2 beef stock cubes
   dissolved in 400ml
   boiling water
10 mangetout
4 tsp reduced-salt soy
   sauce
rock salt
cracked black pepper

Start by sautéing your meatballs in a non-stick pan until they are sealed and brown. Add in your onion, garlic, chilli and mushrooms. Once these are softened, add in your chopped tomatoes, passata, butter beans and the hot stock. Simmer lightly for 35 minutes.

At the end pop in your mangetout (don't overcook them as you want them to retain their crunch). Finally add in your soy sauce and season with some rock salt and cracked black pepper.

10 MINS   **55 MINS**   **3**

CAJUN-STYLE PORK FILLET
WITH AN APPLE AND CARROT SLAW

├────────────────┤

This is a tasty dish that isn't too filling and can also be used as a light lunch.
Swap the ciabatta for potatoes to make this recipe gluten free.

├────────────────┤

Preheat your oven to 180°C.

Sprinkle the Cajun spices on a plastic board and roll your pork fillet in them so it is well coated all over. Wrap in tin foil and pop into the preheated oven to roast for 25 minutes.

To make your slaw, mix your carrot, apple, mayonnaise and parsley in a bowl.

When the pork is nearly ready, pop your ciabatta loaf in the hot oven for a few minutes to warm and crisp up.

Serve the pork in slices with the slaw and warm ciabatta.

1 medium pork fillet,
  trimmed of all visible fat
2 tsp Cajun spices
1 carrot, grated
1 Granny Smith apple,
  peeled cored and grated
15g light mayonnaise
a handful of fresh parsley,
  chopped
1 ciabatta loaf

10 MINS   **35 MINS**   **2**

PAN-FRIED STEAK

———————

Cooking steak can be the hardest thing in the world when you do not know how to, so I'm going to show you my simple but foolproof method. The key to making sure that a steak is done well is the pan (which should be non-stick and ovenproof).

———————

1 lean fillet steak
salt and black pepper
oil for frying
1 sprig of rosemary
3 garlic cloves, sliced

Preheat your oven to 200°C.

Season your steak on both sides well – remember that you will lose 70% of your seasoning the minute it hits the pan.

Heat up an ovenproof pan and add in just a drop of oil – once it hits the heat, it will double. Pop in your steak, rosemary and garlic. Push the steak away from you – you should hear a good sound of sizzling. Seal on one side for 30 seconds without touching it. Do not agitate. Turn it over and repeat. Seal all the edges quickly.

Pop the pan into the warm oven for 4 minutes, then take out and let it rest and relax for 3 minutes.

The more you like your steak cooked, the longer you leave in the oven.

1 MIN   7 MINS   1

LAMB BURGERS
WITH TZATZIKI AND A RED PEPPER ROCKET SALAD

The simplicity of this burger is so appealing. When buying your mince make sure that it is less than 5% fat as this will keep your calories low.

400g lean lamb mince
1 tsp paprika
25g breadcrumbs
2 red onions, finely diced
1 free range egg
50g fresh mint, chopped
salt and black pepper
4 toasted burger buns (optional)

For the tzatziki:
½ a cucumber, grated (don't use the
   middle, seedy part as it is too moist)
100g natural yoghurt
2 tsp chopped fresh mint
juice of ½ a lemon
1 garlic clove, chopped
a pinch of sea salt

For the salad:
100g rocket leaves, washed
6 black olives, stoned
8 gherkins, chopped
1 red pepper, deseeded and chopped
house dressing (see page 192)

Preheat your oven to 180°C.

In a bowl mix your lamb mince, paprika, breadcrumbs, onions, egg, mint and salt and pepper. Make sure everything is mixed completely – you may want to use your (clean) hands to do this!

Shape the mixture into burger shapes and fry on both sides on a hot pan to seal. Finish on a baking tray in the preheated oven for 20 minutes.

To make your tzatziki, get the moisture out of the grated cucumber by squeezing well over the sink. Mix in a bowl with the yoghurt, mint, lemon juice and garlic. Add some sea salt to taste.

Assemble your salad by tossing the ingredients together in a bowl with some house dressing.

When your burgers are done, serve with the salad and tzatziki on the side. You can also serve with layers of tomato, lettuce and onion in a toasted bun.

TRISHA'S TIP

You can have these prepped in advance: just freeze the uncooked patties. Pop some parchment paper in between them so they can be defrosted easily.

10 MINS **30 MINS** **4**

CHICKEN AND TARRAGON BROTH

This is a lovely winter warmer perfect for either lunch or dinner. You can remove the baby potatoes and serve with rice if you would like to change it up.

olive oil

4 boneless, skinless
   chicken thighs

2 chicken stock cubes

700ml water

1 onion, chopped

1 stick of celery, chopped

2 carrots, chopped

1 garlic clove, chopped

10 baby potatoes

a bunch of fresh tarragon,
   chopped (reserve some
   for garnish)

50g frozen peas

salt and black pepper

Heat a stew pot on the hob and sear your chicken in some oil until turning golden. Crumble in your stock cubes and pour in the water, mixing everything well.

Add in your onion, celery, carrots, garlic and baby potatoes. Bring to the boil, then add the tarragon.

Simmer for 15 minutes until the chicken is cooked. Stir in your frozen peas until heated through, then season with salt and pepper.

Serve in bowls, with some more fresh tarragon sprinkled on top.

5 MINS   **15 MINS**   **4**

CHICKEN STUFFED
WITH GARLIC CREAM CHEESE AND WRAPPED IN TURKEY RASHERS

This is a classic, yummy dinner. It is so tasty and so filling and simple.
You can have these prepared the night before you want to eat them.
Just store in the fridge and they'll be ready to rock at dinner time!

2 boneless, skinless
  chicken breasts
100g light cream cheese
2 tsp garlic purée
a handful of fresh parsley,
  chopped
2 turkey rashers

Preheat your oven to 180°C.

To make the stuffing, mix your cheese and garlic purée in a bowl with the parsley.

Create a small incision in each chicken breast, push the stuffing in and cover back with the chicken. Roll each chicken breast in a turkey rasher and bake on a baking tray in the preheated oven for 25 minutes.

This is lovely served on a bed of roasted peppers, onions and courgettes, or just with a green salad.

10 MINS   **25 MINS**   **2**

SESAME CHICKEN
WITH BASMATI RICE

This sticky, tasty dish tastes every bit as good as a Chinese takeaway.
It is a one-pot wonder apart from the rice, which you can get in a microwaveable
pack to make prep even easier! Great for dinner and also reheats well for the next
day's dinner or lunch. One of my favourites!

Cook your rice as per packet instructions.

In a wok, heat 1 teaspoon of the sesame oil. Add in your chicken and carrots and sauté until the chicken is cooked through.

In a bowl, mix the remaining teaspoon of sesame oil with the honey, garlic, sesame seeds, soy sauce, chilli, ginger and spring onions. Toss this into your chicken mixture in the wok and stir for 5 minutes until it becomes sticky. Serve with the rice. Some steamed broccoli is also nice with this.

- 100g basmati rice
- 2 tsp sesame oil
- 4 boneless, skinless chicken breasts, chopped
- 2 carrots, chopped
- 2 tsp honey
- 2 garlic cloves, crushed
- 4 tsp sesame seeds
- 4 tsp reduced-salt soy sauce
- 1 red chilli, chopped
- 2 tsp frozen ginger (or a thumb-sized piece of fresh ginger, peeled and chopped)
- 3 spring onions, finely chopped

7 MINS   **15 MINS**   **4**

CHICKEN TIKKA
WITH BASMATI RICE

I love to make this fragrant takeaway favourite at home for lunch or dinner. You can prepare it all in one pot and it will suit the whole family as the spice level is moderate!

75g basmati rice

olive oil

2 onions, diced

2 tsp frozen garlic (or 2 garlic cloves, chopped)

2 tsp frozen ginger (or a thumb-sized piece of fresh ginger, peeled and chopped)

2 boneless, skinless chicken breasts, chopped

1 red pepper, deseeded and diced

½ tsp ground coriander

½ tsp turmeric

½ tsp paprika

½ tsp ground cumin

½ tsp cracked black pepper

½ tsp curry powder

½ tsp garam masala

1 400g tin of chopped tomatoes

75ml light cream

To garnish:

3 tbsp natural yoghurt

a handful of fresh mint leaves, chopped

Start by putting on your basmati rice to cook according to packet instructions.

Heat a medium-sized non-stick pan and add some oil. Sauté off your onions, garlic and ginger until softened. Add your chicken pieces and stir fry until cooked through. Add in the diced red pepper and stir to combine.

Next tip in all your spices and lightly fry so that the fragrances get released.

Add in your tomatoes and simmer lightly for 5 minutes, then finish by stirring through your cream.

Serve with the rice, and garnish with some natural yoghurt and fresh mint.

5 MINS   **20 MINS**   **2**

CAJUN CHICKEN BREASTS

These are a great staple in my kitchen and are so quick and easy to prepare. I usually make them on a Sunday, to be kept in the fridge and used during the week in dishes like my quesadillas (see page 129). You can simply have them in a sandwich or with a salad, or make a dinner by adding a baked potato or some rice, or stirring them through pasta with some marinara sauce and parsley.

4 boneless, skinless
  chicken breasts
100ml of water
25g Cajun spices

Preheat your oven to 200°C.

Pop your chicken breasts in a baking tray that has sides and coat them all over with the Cajun spices. Pour the water into the tray – this will create steam and keep your chicken moist.

Cook in the preheated oven for 30 minutes, cutting through the thickest part of the chicken at the end to make sure it is cooked through.

If not using straight away, pop into a tub and keep in the fridge for up to 3 days.

3 MINS　**30 MINS**　**4**

CHICKEN, PEPPER AND COURGETTE SKEWERS
WITH HONEY AND SOY SAUCE

I love this as a nice dinner with some salad and hummus, or you can serve it with some rice to make it more filling. You'll need four wooden skewers – soak them in boiling water beforehand to prevent them from splintering or burning.

2 boneless, skinless chicken breasts, chopped into large chunks

3 red peppers, deseeded and chopped into chunks

2 red onions, chopped into chunks

1 courgette, chopped into chunks

For the sauce:

5 tsp honey

6 tsp reduced-salt soy sauce

Preheat the oven to 180°C.

Pop a pot of water on the boil and poach your chicken until cooked. Remove and cool slightly.

To assemble your skewers, pop a piece of chicken, followed by some red pepper, onion and courgette on each one. Continue until all skewers are filled.

Mix the honey with the soy sauce in a small bowl, then brush this mixture all over the skewers, making sure everything is covered. Pop on a tray lined with some tinfoil and roast in the preheated oven for 15 minutes.

5 MINS   **35 MINS**   **2**

SMOKED TURKEY RASHER AND MUSHROOM CARBONARA

Who doesn't love a good, luxurious carbonara? I've brought the fat content of this comfort dish down a notch by substituting turkey rashers for the usual bacon. Great as a dinner dish, this also reheats well for lunch or dinner the next day.

350g tagliatelle

1 tsp oil

2 shallots, diced

6 garlic cloves, minced

15 button mushrooms, halved

6 smoked turkey rashers, chopped

50ml light cream

100g light cream cheese

1 tsp mustard powder

a bunch of fresh, flat leaf parsley, chopped (reserve some for garnish)

salt and black pepper

Cook the pasta as per packet instructions.

In a wok lightly fry your shallots and garlic in the oil. Once these are golden brown add in your mushrooms and turkey rashers.

When the rashers are cooked add in your cream, cream cheese and mustard powder. Stir well to combine.

Fold in your drained pasta and chopped parsley and season with some salt and pepper.

Serve in bowls with some more fresh parsley sprinkled over each serving.

5 MINS **20 MINS** **4**

PESTO & CHERRY TOMATO PASTA

When I have the time, I make my pesto (see page 190) but I often buy pesto in Aldi – it is good value and delicious! This dinner will take only 10 minutes to prepare and it is so yummy!

300g penne pasta
4 garlic cloves
12 cherry tomatoes
1 tsp olive oil
150g pesto
salt and black pepper

Boil your penne in a pot as per packet instructions.

In a medium-sized pan sauté off your garlic and chopped cherry tomatoes in the oil until softened and the tomatoes are breaking up.

Drain your penne and mix into your tomato mixture. Bind your dish with the pesto, making sure it's warmed through, and season. Serve in bowls.

4 MINS   **15 MINS**   **4**

SOUTHERN FRIED CHICKEN

How gorgeous is crispy chicken? Sometimes I miss the deep-fried aspect of my old lifestyle, but I've managed to create a healthy, oven-baked version that is equally gorgeous. This is perfect on its own with some oven-roast chips, my healthy mayonnaise (see page 186) and some salad. You can also chop up and pop in a wrap for lunch!

Preheat your oven to 200°C.

First, butterfly your chicken. With a sharp knife, cut horizontally into your chicken breast to divide it in half, but stopping about 2cm from the opposite side. Open out the breast flat, so it resembles a butterfly.

In a shallow bowl, whisk your egg, water and garlic purée. Mix all your dry ingredients in a separate bowl.

Using one hand, dip your chicken in the egg mixture. Keep the other hand dry. Then pop the chicken in the seasoned flour and coat fully. Place on some kitchen paper to get ready to put into the oven.

With your dry hand, place your coated chicken on a baking sheet and cook in the preheated oven for 15 minutes.

1 chicken breast
1 free range egg
a drop of water
½ tsp garlic purée
5 tsp coconut flour
1 tsp smoked paprika
1 tsp Cajun spices
1 tsp ground turmeric

5 MINS   15 MINS   1

CHICKEN STIR-FRY

Can you beat this dish really? It is nutritious, colourful, easy to prepare and great to keep your calories at bay! Packet sauces can be very high in calories so it's so much better to make your own. Make sure your wok is at a high heat to keep your veg crunchy. Don't add them in too soon!

150g basmati rice

2 tsp sesame oil

2 boneless, skinless chicken breasts, chopped

1 red onion, chopped

2 garlic cloves, chopped

1 red chilli, chopped

a splash of water

1 red pepper, deseeded and chopped

1 carrot, cut into thin strips (julienned)

1 inch of fresh ginger, peeled and chopped

50g mangetout, chopped

100g tenderstem broccoli, chopped

2 tsp reduced-salt soy sauce

2 tsp sriracha sauce

a bunch of fresh coriander, chopped

4 spring onions, chopped

Start by putting your rice on to cook according to packet instructions.

Heat your wok and add in your sesame oil. Fry the chicken, onion, garlic and chilli. Add a splash of water at this point to create steam! When the chicken is cooked add in your pepper, carrot, ginger, mangetout and broccoli. Toss around for 4 minutes.

Next add in your soy sauce and sriracha and mix around. Finish by stirring in your cooked rice. Add in your fresh coriander and spring onions and serve!

5 MINS **20 MINS** **2**

HOMEMADE PIZZA

|————|

A friday night pizza done quick and easy.
After a hard week's work, this is exactly what the doctor ordered!

|————|

1 tsp olive oil

1 spring onion, chopped

2 mushrooms, chopped

3 turkey rashers chopped

2 garlic flatbreads (available from your supermarket)

50ml marinara sauce (see page 189)

25g mozzarella, chopped

5 black olives, chopped

To garnish:
fresh basil sprigs
pine nuts, toasted
chilli flakes (optional)

Preheat your oven to 220°C.

Lightly fry your spring onion, mushrooms and rashers in a non-stick pan with the olive oil until cooked.

Spread your marinara sauce evenly on the flatbreads and then arrange your fried mix on top. Scatter over the mozzarella and olives.

Pop into the oven for 12–14 minutes. When the pizza comes out sprinkle your basil leaves and toasted pine nuts on top and some chilli flakes if you like it spicy.

5 MINS   **20 MINS**   **2**

TRISHA'S TIP

A homemade pizza is a
fun activity that all the
family can be involved in.

ROAST HAKE
WITH A HAM AND PETITS POIS SALSA

Hake is a beautiful, versatile fish that will take on the flavour of its accompaniments so well. It has a subtle flavour and is kind on the palate. Ham and petits pois combine with the zestiness of the lemon to make this an incredibly flavoursome dish!

2 pieces of fresh hake, all
    bones removed
olive oil
salt and black pepper
a squeeze of lemon juice

For the salsa:
50g good-quality butcher
    ham, shredded
50g frozen petits pois
2 tsp lemon juice
a handful of fresh mint
    leaves, chopped (reserve
    some sprigs to garnish)

To garnish:
lemon wedges

Preheat your oven to 200°C.

Pop your hake on a baking tray lined with baking parchment. Drizzle over some olive oil and season with salt, pepper and a squeeze of lemon juice. Pop your tray into the preheated oven and roast the hake for 15 minutes.

To make the salsa, heat a pan, add a drop of oil and sauté off your ham. Let the ham crisp up so it nearly starts to caramelise.

Add in your frozen petits pois and let the heat of the pan defrost them. Finish off with your lemon juice and chopped mint.

Serve your hake garnished with some lemon wedges and some fresh mint leaves, with the salsa on the side.

5 MINS   **25 MINS**   **2**

SHRIMP AND PEA FRIED RICE

I generally prefer basmati rice but brown rice will work with this recipe too. A great thing about this dish is that you can make it for dinner and take it to work with you for lunch the very next day. If you plan to do this, make sure you chill it within 90 minutes of making it and only reheat it once.

75g basmati rice

1 tsp sesame oil

1 onion, diced

2 garlic cloves, crushed

1 red chilli, diced

100g uncooked frozen shrimps or prawns

1 red pepper, deseeded and diced

25g frozen petits pois

2 tsp reduced-salt soy sauce

1 spring onion, chopped

a bunch of fresh coriander, chopped

To garnish:
lime wedges

Boil your rice in a pot as per packet instructions.

Heat a wok, add the sesame oil and lightly fry off your onions, garlic and chilli until softened.

Add in your frozen shrimps/prawns and red pepper and stir. Once the shrimps have defrosted add in your cooked rice, frozen petits pois and soy sauce.

Toss around for 3 minutes and then add in your chopped spring onion and coriander.

Garnish with a lime wedge.

7 MINS   **20 MINS**   **2**

CURRIED CAULIFLOWER RISOTTO

This hearty, flavourful dish makes a lovely veggie dinner on its own, or you can add some chicken or pan–fried fish on top to make it more substantial. The key to a good risotto is to add your liquid slowly and allow the rice to swell.

1 tbsp olive oil

1 onion, diced

4 sticks of celery, chopped

2 garlic cloves, chopped

3 tsp curry powder

300g arborio rice

1 medium head of
   cauliflower, chopped
   into small pieces (slice a
   piece off for garnish first)

2 reduced-salt vegetable
   stock cubes dissolved in 1
   litre of boiling water

salt and black pepper

To garnish:

a small handful of fresh
   coriander, chopped

1 spring onion, chopped

Heat the oil in a medium-sized pan and lightly cook off your onion, celery and garlic until well softened.

Add your curry powder and cook until the fragrant smell wafts up. Add in your rice and stir to coat in the oil. Stir through your cauliflower.

Gradually add some hot stock and stir. Once the rice has absorbed the liquid, add some more liquid and continue on until the stock is gone. Season with salt and pepper.

Quickly pan fry your reserved cauliflower slice. Garnish each dish with the cauliflower slice, spring onion and coriander.

5 MINS   **20 MINS**   **4**

TRISHA'S TIP

Always stop cooking before
the risotto goes soft so that
it is al dente.

BEETROOT AND GOAT'S CHEESE RISOTTO

This staple dish from the restaurant is just so yummy and comforting.
If you remove the cheese it is also vegan friendly!

4 bulbs of cooked beetroot
1 tbsp olive oil
1 onion, diced
2 sticks of celery, chopped
2 garlic cloves, chopped
300g arborio rice
800ml hot vegetable stock
100ml white wine
salt and black pepper
1 bunch of fresh parsley,
    chopped (reserve some
    for garnish)
juice of 1 lemon
15g goat's cheese

Blitz your beetroot with a stick blender in a jug with a drop of water to make a bright pink paste.

Heat the oil in a medium-sized pan and lightly cook off your onion, celery and garlic until well softened. Add in your rice and stir to coat in the oil.

Mix your stock and wine together in a jug and slowly begin to add this liquid to the rice. Keep adding in a bit of wine and stock bit by bit, stirring constantly, until the rice has absorbed the liquid and swelled and is cooked al dente (retaining a slight crunch). Season with salt and pepper.

Stir through your beetroot paste, along with most of the chopped parsley and the lemon juice. Crumble over the goat's cheese and some parsley.

5 MINS   **20 MINS**   **4**

FISH CAKES

My secret ingredient to a good fish cake? Tinned salmon! I know it isn't the most cheffy thing in the world but I have found that it makes a more stable fish cake and it isn't as wet when it is a finished product. I love these served with oven-baked chips and some peas. For a lighter meal, you could also enjoy them with a peppery rocket salad. Having the mash made ahead of time makes these very easy to pull together!

Preheat your oven to 180°C.

First get your bowls ready to dip your shaped fish cakes in before frying. Beat the eggs in one shallow bowl with a splash of water. Put your breadcrumbs in another shallow bowl together with the lemon zest. Throw the flour into a third bowl.

Now you're ready to make your fish cakes. In a large bowl mix your mash, salmon, chives, cayenne pepper and salt and pepper.

Sprinkle some flour on a clean work surface or chopping board. Grab handfuls of the spud and fish mixture and shape into four even fish cakes.

Dip each fish cake first into your flour, then your egg then your zesty breadcrumbs, shaking off excess coating after each one.

Heat your frying pan and add some oil. Lightly fry your fish cakes on each side until they become golden brown and then pop them into the oven for 15 minutes.

Serve with some Thai mayonnaise (see page 186) and some rocket salad or oven-baked chips.

2 free range eggs
a splash of water
40g fine breadcrumbs
zest of 1 lemon
a handful of flour
4 medium potatoes, peeled, boiled and mashed until there are no lumps
400g tinned salmon, drained
100g fresh chives, chopped
2 tsp cayenne pepper
salt and black pepper
oil, for frying

25 MINS   **5 MINS**   **4**

SAUCES, DRESSINGS & SIDES

The danger is in the dose! Take it from me, when eating out, sauces are LETHAL. As executive head chef in a busy kitchen I know exactly how much butter a kitchen will go through to make its sauces taste good. Okay, they're delicious but could mess up your weight loss and motivation big time if you have too much of them. So my tactic is to always order my sauce on the side, never on top. As for sides, they can also be fraught with danger – the temptation of chips or onion rings or creamy coleslaw is immense. I personally order a baked potato, salad or some steamed broccoli instead. I'd choose brown soda bread with my soup as opposed to a bread roll; roast potatoes as opposed to mash – you've no idea how much butter went into making that mash! I don't leave anything to chance now – when I'm ordering I make sure I know EXACTLY what is coming my way.

  PREP TIME

 COOKING TIME

 SERVES

V **VEGETARIAN**

 GF **GLUTEN FREE**

HEALTHY MAYONNAISE THREE WAYS

Mayo is my vice; I absolutely love it but sadly the stuff is loaded in calories!
So, I have created this alternative, healthy swap. This will last in your fridge for
three days and the more flavours you add in the less it tastes like yoghurt!
It couldn't be easier – I just take some natural yoghurt and add in various
flavours. You could experiment with your own!

1. LEMON AND CHIVE

50g natural yoghurt
juice of ½ a lemon
a few fresh chives, snipped
1 tsp soy sauce

2. GARLIC

50g natural yoghurt
2 tsp garlic purée

3. THAI

50g natural yoghurt
1 tsp sesame oil
1 tsp soy sauce

Just mix your choice of mayo in a small bowl and serve as a dip, spread or salad dressing.

5 MINS   **2 PORTIONS**

CAESAR DRESSING

———————

This is my healthy take on the classic Caesar dressing. I promise you it is as nice as any Caesar dressing you'll get in a restaurant.
Try my Caesar salad recipe on page 120 and you'll see what I mean!

———————

100g natural yoghurt

30g Parmesan cheese, grated

3 tsp reduced-salt soy sauce

2 garlic cloves, chopped or
    2 tsp frozen garlic

Combine all the ingredients in a bowl and mix. If not using immediately, cover with a lid or cling film and pop in the fridge, where it will keep for up to three days. Always give it a good stir before use.

5 MINS   **8 PORTIONS**

MARINARA SAUCE

In case you haven't guessed yet from the amount of recipes I use this in (Bolognese, page 147, Healthy Baked Beans, page 134) this rich Italian sauce is a huge favourite of mine. Make yourself a batch of this on a Sunday and use it all week long.

Heat a medium-sized pan and give it three sprays of oil, or add some olive oil. Lightly sauté your red onions and garlic until sizzling and translucent.

Next add in your passata, veg stock, salt, pepper and basil and simmer for 10 minutes. Then add in your balsamic vinegar and simmer for a further 2 minutes.

To finish, blitz your sauce until velvet-smooth with a stick blender. Chill and store for up to three days in your fridge, or freeze individual portions.

spray oil/olive oil
2 red onions, chopped
4 garlic cloves, chopped
1 500g carton of passata
1 reduced-salt vegetable
   stock cube dissolved in
   100ml boiling water
salt and black pepper
3 tsp frozen or dried basil
25ml balsamic vinegar

5 MINS   **15 MINS**   **6 PORTIONS**

GREEN PESTO

⊢————————⊣

There is just nothing like the smell of fresh pesto! This can be used for an easy midweek meal with pasta (see page 170). It's also great as a spread.

⊢————————⊣

100g fresh basil leaves
50g grated Parmesan
120ml extra virgin olive oil
50g toasted pine nuts
2 garlic cloves
sea salt and black pepper

Pop everything into a bowl and blitz until a smooth paste. If you want to freeze, leave out the Parmesan and freeze in ice-cube trays.

7 MINS   8 PORTIONS

DRESSINGS FOUR WAYS

The hardest part of a salad is getting flavour in there so it's not just boring rabbit food! But when your core ingredients are fresh and crunchy and you have a banger of a dressing it all comes together. The key to a good salad for me is crunch, and having certain parts of the salad hot, like your protein. In college we were always taught that dressing should be a 3:1 ratio. So it should be three parts oil or yoghurt to one part of the flavour (vinegar, lemon juice, etc). Always remember that a dressing is a temporary emulsion, so before each use shake your bottle to mix up what has separated. The Thai dressing at the end is higher in fat so use it more sparingly than the others. When measuring small amounts of liquid, don't forget that 5ml is equivalent to one teaspoon.

1 HOUSE DRESSING
(or vinaigrette)
60ml extra virgin olive oil
20ml sherry vinegar
salt and black pepper

2 BALSAMIC DRESSING
60ml extra virgin olive oil
20ml balsamic vinegar
salt and black pepper

3 LEMON DRESSING
60ml extra virgin olive oil
20ml lemon juice
salt and black pepper

4 THAI DRESSING
60ml sesame oil
20ml soy sauce
10ml sriracha sauce
5ml Thai fish sauce (nam pla)

Just mix the ingredients for your choice of the above dressings in a clean, screw-top jar. Put the lid on tightly and shake it up. They will last happily in the fridge for two weeks.

3 MINS   5 PORTIONS

STUFFED PORTOBELLO MUSHROOMS

These make a lovely side to a dinner instead of your regular vegetables, or you could eat them as part of your breakfast or add a simple salad for a lunchtime dish. These are not the best reheated so in this scenario fresh is best!

Preheat your oven to 180°C.

Cut the stalks out of your mushrooms so that they are easy to stuff.

Roast your pine nuts on a baking tray in the oven for a few minutes until they are golden brown. Don't take your eyes off them – they can burn very easily!

In a pot melt your butter and slowly stew your diced onion until translucent. Mix in your breadcrumbs and take off the heat. Mix in your blue cheese and tightly stuff your raw mushrooms with the mixture. Pop them on a baking tray and into the oven for 15 minutes until golden and crispy. Serve with the roasted pine nuts sprinkled over.

2 Portobello mushrooms
5g pine nuts
10g butter
1 onion, diced
20g fresh breadcrumbs
15g blue cheese

5 MINS   **15 MINS**   **2**

SAUTÉED TENDERSTEM BROCCOLI
WITH GARLIC AND SEA SALT

|—————————|

This is an ideal, easy-to-make snack or a side for your dinner.
The key is to blanch the broccoli in ice-cold water to stop the cooking
and to keep its lovely bright green colour.

|—————————|

200g tenderstem broccoli
1 tsp olive oil
3 tsp frozen garlic (or 3
    garlic cloves, chopped)
sea salt

Blanch your broccoli by following the instructions on page 106.

Heat a wok and add in your olive oil and garlic. Toss your tenderstem broccoli in the garlicky oil for 2 minutes. Sprinkle with your sea salt and serve.

5 MINS   **2 MINS**   **2**

ROASTED ROOT VEGETABLES

This nutritious and colourful dish can be used as a side to your dinner or on its own as a delicious snack. It's important to cut your veg into similar-sized pieces so they will all cook at the same rate.

1 carrot, chopped

1 parsnip, chopped

1 sweet potato, peeled and cut into cubes

2 tsp olive oil

3 garlic cloves, chopped

1 sprig of fresh thyme

a drizzle of honey

Preheat your oven to 200°C.

Put your prepared veg in a bowl and toss with the olive oil and garlic, making sure everything is well coated. Spread out evenly onto a baking tray and pop the sprig of thyme on top. Roast in the preheated oven for 35 minutes, turning them once. At the end, drizzle in some honey, sprinkle with thyme and serve.

5 MINS   **35 MINS**   **2**

THYME AND GARLIC ROASTED POTATOES

——————

Spuds are a staple in every home! They are so yummy and I do not believe that you have to lose potatoes to lose weight!

——————

10 baby potatoes

3 tsp olive oil

8 garlic cloves, chopped

8 sprigs of fresh thyme,
    leaves stripped

salt and black pepper

Preheat the oven to 190°C.

Wash and halve the potatoes.

Parboil the potatoes until they are half cooked (about 10 minutes). Drain in a colander.

Spread them out on a baking tray and drizzle in olive oil, sprinkle your chopped garlic and thyme on top. Sprinkle over the salt and pepper and mix everything together to make sure your spuds are well coated in the oil.

Roast for 25 minutes in the oven, turning regularly to make sure they get golden and crispy all over.

10 MINS   **35 MINS**   **4**

SWEET POTATO MASH

|———|

Sweet potatoes live up to their name – they are sweet and delicious. Their gorgeous vibrant colour makes this much more exciting than regular mash! They are rich in Vitamin C, B and potassium. Perfect as a side to your main dinner dish.

|———|

4 medium sweet potatoes, peeled and cut into big chunks

15g butter

50ml low fat milk

2 sprigs of fresh thyme, leaves chopped

salt and pepper

In a pot cook your potatoes in boiling water until they become soft (about 25 minutes).

Drain your potatoes in a colander and transfer to a bowl. Fold in your butter, milk and chopped thyme and mash until smooth. Season with some salt and pepper and serve.

5 MINS   **25 MINS**   **4**

SHREDDED APPLE, CARROT AND SESAME COLESLAW

Crunchy, fresh and full of flavour! The addition of Granny Smith apples gives a lovely sharp edge to this coleslaw. A perfect side to your pan-fried fillet steak (see page 154).

2 carrots, grated

2 Granny Smith apples, peeled, cored and grated

100g natural yoghurt

3 tsp sesame seeds, toasted in a dry pan until fragrant

salt and black pepper

a small handful of fresh coriander, chopped

In a bowl mix your grated carrot and apple into the yoghurt.

Add in your cooled sesame seeds and season with salt and pepper.

Stir in the fresh coriander and serve. This will last for a couple of days in your fridge.

10 MINS   **2**

ROASTED BRUSSELS SPROUTS

———

Brussels sprouts? They're not just for Christmas! And definitely not just to be boiled and overcooked! Love them or hate them, this dish is so tasty. It's time to show them some love. Blanching the sprouts before roasting means they keep their lovely green colour.

———

200g Brussels sprouts, trimmed and halved
75g smoky bacon, chopped
1 red onion, diced
50g crushed walnuts
1 tbsp balsamic vinegar
salt and black pepper
1 tsp lemon juice

Preheat your oven to 200°C.

First you need to blanch your sprouts. Get a bowl of ice-cold water ready. Bring a pot of salted water to a boil and add your sprouts. Once the water comes back to a rapid boil remove the sprouts and pop them in the bowl of ice-cold water. Drain.

On a roasting tray spread out your blanched sprouts, bacon, red onion and walnuts and toss in the balsamic vinegar. Season with salt and pepper.

Pop into your preheated oven for 12 minutes. Drizzle over the lemon juice and serve.

5 MINS   **20 MINS**   **4**

COUSCOUS

———

Couscous is one of the most versatile ingredients around: it will adapt to whatever flavour you put with it. Here I will show you how to make the basic couscous, which is like a blank canvas for so many flavours. Below are a few of my favourites.

———

200g couscous
1 reduced-salt vegetable
   stock cube dissolved in
   300ml boiling water
1 sprig of fresh thyme

Put the dried couscous in a bowl and have some cling film to hand. Pour the hot stock over the dried couscous, add your sprig of thyme and cover securely with cling film. Leave this sit for 5 minutes.

Remove the cling film and fluff up with a fork.

1 TOMATO AND BASIL

Mix a handful of cherry tomatoes and some torn, fresh basil through your couscous.

2 PEA AND HAM

Cook 50g of frozen peas and stir through your couscous with 2 slices of shop-bought honey-roast ham, shredded.

3 BEETROOT AND GOAT'S CHEESE

I usually buy my beetroot cooked in the veg section of Aldi so I would suggest getting one beet and dicing it up finely before stirring through the couscous. Finish by crumbling 15g of goat's cheese on top.

5 MINS   **7 MINS**   **2**

GREEN OLIVE TAPENADE

This is one of my favourite sauces – or is it a dip or a spread? There is a lovely, earthy Mediterranean flavour from the olives, capers, olive oil and herbs. Great as a topping for bruschetta (see also page 138), as a dip with some crudités or swirled through pasta.

Blitz all the ingredients in a blender until smooth. Taste to see if you need to add more lemon juice. Store in the fridge for up to three days.

120g green olives, pitted

40g almonds

1 bunch of fresh basil

1 bunch of fresh mint leaves

60ml olive oil

2 tbsp lemon juice

4 anchovy fillets

1 tbsp capers

6 MINS   **4**

SUNDRIED TOMATO AND BASIL WHITE SODA BREAD

├────────────┤

This is a favourite in the restaurant, you can pop some real butter on this and enjoy it as a treat. You can also freeze it and use it for toast!

├────────────┤

425g plain flour
1 tsp salt
1 tsp bread soda
1 bunch of fresh basil, chopped
50g semi-sundried tomatoes, chopped
350ml buttermilk

Preheat your oven to 180°C.

Combine all the ingredients in a bowl and mix gently into a dough – do not overwork it as it will become tough.

Shape your mixture into a mound and place into a lightly oiled loaf tin. Use a knife to draw a cross in the centre. Sprinkle some more salt on top.

Bake in the preheated oven for 45 minutes. Remove, turn the bread upside-down and return to the oven to cook for another 10 minutes. Leave to cool on a wire rack.

I advise you to cut it and freeze it when it is cool as you will be tempted to overeat on this one! That way, you can defrost one slice at a time.

10 MINS   55 MINS   10 SLICES

SPINACH AND ROCKET SALAD
WITH POMEGRANATE

├────────────┤

This simple salad can be eaten alone or served as a side to one of your dishes.
You can make this ahead and have it ready, adding your house dressing
at the last minute – any earlier, and your salad will go limp.

├────────────┤

20g almonds

70g rocket, washed

70g baby spinach, washed

seeds from 1 pomegranate

30g feta cheese, crumbled

1 tbsp house dressing
   (see page 192)

Toast your almonds in a dry frying pan over a medium heat
until golden brown and fragrant – about 5 minutes.

Mix all the ingredients (apart from the dressing) together in a
bowl. If serving straight away, pour over the dressing and toss
to coat all elements of the salad.

10 MINS   2

SNACKS

I don't know do I love these or hate these. If I batch cook protein balls the chances of me eating them all are fairly high. I won't have the willpower to just have one with my cup of tea so I will often make smaller batches to use as a buffer in between my meals to stop me from getting hangry. Here are my top tips for snacking. When you are in a garage or a coffee shop, avoid getting pre-packed rolls and sugary coffees and steer clear of the sweets at the till. I often have some grapes in my hand if I am in a shop so I don't get silly and pick at sweets. I've perfected my technique so much that if I'm travelling to Dublin now, I generally have the car full of petrol the night before as it will stop me from stopping at a shop and picking up sweets!

PREP TIME

COOKING TIME

SERVES

VEGETARIAN

GLUTEN FREE

HUMMUS

├────────────┤

This is a great dip to have in the fridge. You can either use it as a snack with some crudités or you can toast some pitta bread and have it as your lunch. It is vegan friendly, high in protein and a great substitute for mayonnaise.

├────────────┤

1 400g tin of drained
   chickpeas
4 tsp extra virgin olive oil
1 tbsp lime juice
2 tsp ground coriander
1 tsp paprika
salt and black pepper
10g tahini
4 garlic cloves

Pop all of your ingredients in a blender and mix until you have a smooth paste.

10 MINS   6

NUT SLICES

These are a handy snack that can be popped into your handbag.
They are high in healthy fats. Don't overeat these as the calories would
be higher because of the nuts!

100g pitted dates, chopped
80g flaked almonds
150g salted peanuts
45g pumpkin seeds
35g Rice Krispies
1 tsp cinnamon
2 tbsp almond butter
2 tbsp honey
2 tbsp coconut oil

Preheat your oven to 160°C.

Boil your dates for six minutes and mash with a fork.

In a blender, blitz your almonds, peanuts and pumpkin seeds.
Transfer this mixture to a bowl and mix in the Rice Krispies.

Pop your dates, cinnamon, almond butter, honey and coconut
oil into a pot and heat gently until combined, and then add to
the mixing bowl. Mix all the ingredients together.

Using the back of spoon, spread your mix out on a baking sheet
lined with parchment and bake in the preheated oven for 20
minutes.

Allow to cool slightly, then cut into 10 slices. Store in an airtight
container for up to a week.

10 MINS   **35 MINS**   **10 SLICES**

PROTEIN BALLS

├─────────────┤

This is the handiest snack ever! Be careful as they are yummy
and the nut butter is high in fat! They freeze well and
are very nutritious.

├─────────────┤

Simply mix all the ingredients together in a bowl. Using clean hands (you could wet them a bit first to stop the mixture from sticking) roll into balls. Pop them on a tray and into the fridge and leave to set.

Enjoy with a cup of coffee or grab as you run out the door to avoid hunger pangs on the go!

200g smooth 100% peanut butter
300g porridge oats
50g honey
60g chocolate protein powder
50g dark chocolate, finely chopped

20 MINS   **12 BALLS**

ROASTED CHICKPEA BITES

I find these so handy when I am travelling on a long car journey
and I need something to pick on besides high-fat crisps!.
These crispy, protein-packed bites are gorgeous!

1 400g tin of chickpeas,
    drained
1 tsp olive oil
2 tsp paprika
1 tsp cumin seeds
1 tsp curry powder

Preheat your oven to 180°C.

Mix all the ingredients in a bowl, making sure all the chickpeas
are well coated with the oil and spices. Spread out on a baking
tray and pop into your preheated oven for 25 minutes.

Remove, cool down and store in an airtight container. Eat as a
snack on the go or sprinkle over your salads for some crunch.

5 MINS   **25 MINS**   **4**

Acknowledgements

There are so many people I need to thank. I would like to thank my family: my sisters – Brigid, Ellen, Maura, Carol, Michelle, Annie, Kellie and Juliette – you guys are my best friends. I love you very much. Thank you for giving me the most incredible bunch of nieces and nephews. Eva, Eóghain, Will, Pearse, Jack, Lucy, Oran, Dylan, Luke, Amy, Dean and Danny – you guys are my world. To my brothers-in-law, thank you for everything over the years. You are the best gang I could wish for. You rock!

I would like to thank Mam, my queen. I adore the bones of you. You are my best friend. I will never be able to repay you for the way you've minded me. You are the greatest mother in the world. Thank you, Dad, for everything over the years.

Thank you, Emma Ryan, for being an amazing personal trainer and for showing me that I could do it.

Thank you to Jacobs on the Mall and the McCarthy family, who have supported me ever since I walked in the front door in 2007. Tom and Kate have been like parents to me over the last 13 years and have not only given me a job but cared for me, too. Michelle has been the best boss and friend I could ask for. I would like to thank my team in Jacobs: Ricky, Patsy, Jacinta, Shaneen, Ross, William, Thomas and Doc. You are my colleagues and my friends. I will always be grateful for how you looked after me when things were bad.

Thanks also to my work husband, Niall, for always being there for me. A special thank you to Doc and Shaneen, who helped to build my butter towers! A big thank you to all the customers, too, for cheering me on over the last two years.

Thanks to Ryan Tubridy, for giving me the opportunity to meet all my Transformers. Also, thank you to PJ Coogan from 96 FM for giving me my first interview, and to Red FM's Neil Prendeville for his constant support over the last two years. I would like to thank Kathryn Thomas, who's been a huge support to me behind the scenes.

Thank you to Brian Keane, who sat me down and told me I should write a book and for always being an open ear. Paul Dermody always gave me solid advice, too, and makes me smile when he messages.

TRISHA'S TRANSFORMATION

Thanks to Sharon Keegan, from Peachy Lean, who always makes sure I'm dressed right for the gym. She is one in a million. And to New Dimensions for giving me some lovely pants to wear for my photoshoot. Also, thanks to John Buckley Sports for making sure my feet are always in good footwear.

To Laura O'Callaghan, for always being my friend, even though I avoided her wedding. I hope this thank you will fix that! Thanks, Laura, for giving me my Instagram name and for always being my biggest supporter. Also, thanks to Colin McDonnell for giving me the push to start my Instagram.

I would like to thank Sarah, Aoibheann and Teresa at Gill Books, for supporting me and helping me to get this book on the shelves.

Thank you to Gerry and Miriam Hussey. You have always been so kind to me and have provided me with such value and comfort in my life.

Marc O'Sullivan, my photographer for the book, made me feel like a supermodel and so comfortable in front of his camera. Thanks to Annemarie for my amazing make-up on the day of the shoot, as well as Onagh from Platinum Hair, who made me feel so glamorous, and Ronan Dunbar, who styled my hair for the shoot. The whole team on the day were legends.

I would like to thank my friends for always being there for me. A big shout out the to rest of the Sexy Six – Niamh, Colm, Jack Snr, Jack Jnr, Jack Daly. Thank you for always being my friend, even when I was a flake. Cornelia and Aisling, you are my girl-power friends, and to all my friends – I truly adore you.

Thank you to my stylist, Mr Dan Sweeney, who came to Dublin and made sure I was dressed right. Dan has been an awesome friend to me. Thank you, Dan, for always motivating me and encouraging me to be the best possible version of myself. Thank you for filming for me and for always making me laugh. I would like to thank Cathy Sweeney, the best hairdresser and friend I could ask for. Also, thanks to Rebecca and Mary in Reeb, who have been so kind to me over the years, especially in 2017, when things were tough!

Thank you, Zoe, and the gang at City Wax, who always make sure I look as glamorous as I feel, and to Fifth Avenue for making sure my nails are always intact.

I would like to thank my local community in Kilbehenny and Mitchelstown for supporting me from day one and hooting the horn at me when I'm out walking.

Finally, I would like to thank my Transformers. Thank you for buying this book. It's really a dream come true. You guys are simply the best. Beat the bulge!

Index